Readers Respond
to Control Freak

Some may say it takes guts to openly share like TJ does in this book, revealing private trials and struggles. I say "thank you" for inspiring us by making yourself the example that our imperfections can be our gifts.

– Cari Pirello, friend and fellow imperfectionist

The concept of wielding control like a weapon versus yielding control to the Lord has changed my way of thinking forever. TJ challenges his readers as he takes them on a journey through his truly unbelievable life. Be an MVP and read this story!

– Jim Barnard, author of
The Suffering Guy and *Made Alive*

With a raw honesty and transparency that is often lacking in today's climate, TJ Sharitz weaves a compelling story of overwhelming odds, the struggle to control them, and the God who is able to do above and beyond what we could ever imagine.

– Kathryn Cushman, author of
The Plans We Made and *Finding Me*

TJ Sharitz is a storyteller, and his story affirms to Whom we belong, that we are not forsaken, and that our daily life is not the main event nor are we the architect.

– Tony Rich, husband, dad, and aspiring carpenter

We all need grace. This book is written with that in mind from a refreshing personal perspective, by one who is a "product of grace." The author's zest for life is indicative of one who has experienced grace and looks to share it with others. Life is hard and can have a devaluing and devastating impact on us. We need the "seeds of hope, gratitude, and inspiration" that may be implanted in us as described in these beneficial words.

– James Donovan, professor of education, Point University

The **Least** Valuable Player

Control Freak

TJ Sharitz

RETELLING, LLC

Hardcover ISBN 979-8-9905833-0-6
Softcover ISBN 979-8-9905833-1-3
eBook ISBN 979-8-9905833-2-0

Published in association with Retelling, LLC. Retelling.net

Design by Cynthia Young. Youngdesign.biz

Contents

This book is dedicated to both of my earthly fathers.

To my dad, Charlie Sharitz,
who taught me to be honest and a man of integrity and character.

To my father-in-law, John Bieberstein,
who demonstrated how to be a loving father and servant leader.

Foreword

I'VE BEEN FRIENDS WITH TJ since high school. I always admired him on and off the football field. We both shared an interest in radio and becoming disc jockeys, so TJ and I would practice radio in his basement. It was great fun! To me it seemed that TJ had it all: great looks, super athletic, everyone's friend, and a true jock at school. It wasn't until I reconnected with TJ several years ago that I started to learn about his struggles with health and the trials that God had and was taking him through.

Control. It's not just a Janet Jackson song anymore! We all have a tendency to want to control things in our lives. This book will open your eyes to traits that maybe you see in yourself. I love the power of determination that TJ describes through his life, never wanting to quit or settle for less. Even through the let downs or lack of touchdowns, TJ continually pushed himself and sought ways to be better—at controlling his life.

Throughout the book, TJ reflects on how God was actually in control even though he couldn't see it. I have control issues as well. This book dives deep, deep into a couple of really dark secrets that

TJ had been carrying for years, one as a young boy. He attempted to control his life by compartmentalizing things and keeping them hidden from his friends, and more importantly, his family. The powerful awakening that he experienced brought tears to my eyes. TJ opened my eyes to the light that God will shine on my own life if I just allow him to be in the driver's seat. We have a loving Shepherd who's knocking at the door waiting to personally lead you and me on this amazing life journey. The freedom of surrendering to God allows us to open the connection to the Holy Spirit that resides inside of us. He can set us free.

One of my favorite singers is Jeremy Camp and his song "Dead Man Walking" is very much like this book:

> I was a dead man walking
> Until I was a man walking with you
> I was a blind man falling
> Until I felt the life you're calling me to
> Pulling me out of the darkness and
> Pulling me out of the lies
> Putting the beat in my heart again
> I was a dead man walking
> Until you loved this dead man walking back to life
> *–Used by permission of Jeremy Camp*

Through the touchdowns, fumbles, penalties, and time outs, God is the coach grooming you for the truly Big Game. Set yourself free of control. Surrender it all to God and really start living. Put down the remote and let God change the channel for you.

- Tom Sullivan,
corporate events master of ceremonies and television host

Introduction

I AM A RECOVERING CONTROL FREAK. Being a control freak was a way of life. The only way I knew I could survive and thrive. I treated control like it was the most valuable player, the hotshot superstar that could make anything happen. What a joke.

They say in life that "life lessons" are the best teachers, preferably someone else's and not your own. Well, I didn't listen. I had to learn the hard way. Doing things my way, all by myself. So, I became a control freak who craved only one thing: more control. For much of my life, I insisted on controlling everything I could. And by everything, I mean every single thing. Like an addict, I had an unquenchable thirst for control—especially in times when God seemed to be uncaring and absent, like when I was a kid dealing with dyslexia and attention deficit disorder, and a young athlete trying to make my way. I believed that only the perseverance of total control would get me the results I wanted. Until I finally learned Who really is in control. Spoiler alert: it's not me.

Time and time again, control revealed itself to be the least valuable player, threatening to destroy my life instead of playing along with me to achieve what I desired. My life has been an ongoing series of situations that all go to illustrate how destructive control is. One event after another.

A few short years ago I found myself in a living hell where all hope seemed lost. I shouldn't even be alive. No one could have ever dared to dream that I'd get from there to here, not even me. But God was faithful and never let me go.

You will read in my story how I became a control freak, attempting to maintain control of all things and how that really didn't work out in my favor. You will also read how God, in His kindness and love for me (not only for me, but for you as well), carried out a plan so much better than whatever I was trying to accomplish for myself. It has been a hard lesson to learn, especially for someone as hardheaded as me, but I am grateful to have journeyed through it. My life's journey has shown me that control is something we can pursue with only limited success. A truer level of success always comes when we yield control to the One who is actually in control—God. He can be, should be, and frankly, is in control of all things. In His perfect sovereignty, He graciously allows us the gift of free will—the freedom to choose Him or choose to take control on our own.

So, on that note I need to be clear; I still struggle at times with trying to take control over things. It isn't that I don't trust God to provide. It's just that I'm sometimes forgetful about what He has done in the past, and I fail to apply the lessons I've learned.

This is partially why I wanted to write this book. I needed to have a tangible reminder of how God has worked in my life with His perfect and benevolent control, to help me remember to make the right choice the next time I am tempted to pursue control. I hope my story helps you remember as well.

But the main reason I felt compelled to write my story is that maybe someone else might be going through something so difficult, scary, and gut-wrenching that they too have lost all hope. Someone else might feel all alone and tempted to take control of the situation into their own hands. Maybe that is you. That was me, too. My desire is that you can gain comfort and encouragement from my story and that you can learn from my hardheaded mistakes.

Ultimately, this is God's story to plant seeds of hope, gratitude, and inspiration, and to bless all who read these pages.

– TJ

1

National Championship Super Bowl

Count it all joy, my brothers, when you meet trials of various kinds, for you know that the testing of your faith produces steadfastness. And let steadfastness have its full effect, that you may be perfect and complete, lacking in nothing. (James 1:2-4, ESV)

EARLY ON A SUMMER MORNING in June 2000, I lay in bed next to my amazing wife, Jaci (pronounced Jackie), who was sound asleep in dreamland. Without warning, I felt an explosion in my lower back as if I had been stabbed or shot. Crying out in agony I bolted upright in bed, scanning the room for who or what had attacked me.

The sudden pain felt unlike anything I had ever experienced before. Jaci woke up at the noise and attempted to make sense of what was happening at such an early hour. We hardly ever wake up at 5:30 in the morning, so Jaci seemed a bit frustrated that I was causing such a commotion.

"What's going on? Is something wrong? What are you doing?"

"My lower back hurts all of a sudden. It's kind of intense, actually."

I didn't want to tell her I thought I had been shot because that seemed rather implausible. No one was around, and my frantic inventory of my body turned up no amount of blood.

She yawned and rolled back into her pillow. "Rub some Biofreeze on it and go back to sleep. It's too early."

I found this to be a little dismissive of the traumatic event, but I found the cream and rubbed some in like she said. However, the pain only got worse. I couldn't go back to sleep. After several minutes of wrestling and writhing in bed to get comfortable, I decided to get up and get dressed for work.

On my drive to the office, the pain became so unbearable I stopped at an urgent care clinic. I attempted to understate the pain as I signed in, but the intake nurse could tell I was in bad shape. The doctor did an exam and a few tests, then said he couldn't see anything wrong with me. Most likely I had strained my back, he explained, stating that back strains can produce unfathomable pain. He prescribed anti-inflammatory medicine with bedrest. This diagnosis sounded reasonable to me. I had been working at a seminar a few days earlier that required me to do more physical labor than I was used to. I must have simply pushed too hard over those several days. I could accept that.

With the prescription in hand and committing myself to bedrest, I assumed I would improve rather quickly. The following week, however, the pain didn't get better; it continued to get worse. Much worse. I had no idea just how much worse it would get.

Death was coming for me.

The worst part was I had no control over it. And I needed to have control. Complete control. Over everything. I had learned to take control of my own life way back when I was a kid. It all started the day of our very own National Championship Super Bowl when I was nine years old.

On a beautiful summer day in Atlanta, a gentle, almost cool breeze, which is extremely rare in the south, blew over the yard. The sun had not yet heated up the day under the clear blue sky. After my brother and I mowed our front yard, it looked like a brand-new carpet—each blade cut to absolute perfection. Our yard looked just as good, if not better, than any of the fields we watched collegiate or professional athletes play on. I felt so much pride and ownership of our carefully manicured environment, the perfectly cut football field on game day. Instant pride, excitement, and gratification, all in one beautiful moment. That's exactly what my younger brother Jack and I felt that morning.

A lot of this pride came from my dad and his strong drive for things to be a certain way. My dad had a way of pushing me toward maximum effort on certain things. When he first taught my little brother and me how to mow the lawn, he pointed out the areas that didn't look good in the yard: the edging, the lines, the details. He wasn't being nit-picky; he just knew when we hadn't given our best effort.

On this day, however, I knew Dad would be proud of me and my little brother. We'd followed his instructions; the yard looked perfect. I felt invincible, in control, and at the same time excited, anticipating great things to come, knowing how proud and pleased our dad would be.

He and my mom had gone to town while Jack and I worked on the yard. Before they left, our parents gave us permission to invite the neighbor kids over for a football game after we were done with our lawn mowing chores. I wasn't sure where they went or how long they would be gone, but I hoped Dad would be back before we started trampling all over the perfect front yard.

Jack and I took a moment to take in our masterpiece on this perfect day. The smell of freshly cut grass filled the air. You could feel, almost touch, the excitement and anticipation. That moment probably only lasted three seconds, but it still feels significant to this day.

As much as I wanted to wait to start the football game until Dad arrived—with loads of compliments and fanfare for a job well done—I also really wanted to play football. Football was my favorite sport. As a nine-year-old, it was hard to hold off on an opportunity to play.

Once our friends came over, we were ready to kick off for our very own "National Championship Super Bowl." We liked college and pro football equally, so it was obvious to combine the titles together. I called my team the Hokies. The Hokies are the mascot for my favorite team, Virginia Tech. My dad and grandfather both went to school at Virginia Tech, and I dreamed of one day playing college football for the VT Hokies myself.

As we selected our teams for the National Championship Super Bowl, I invited my friend to be a Hokie with me, which didn't excite him, but he knew he had a better chance of winning on my team, so he went with it. I started *gobbling* and doing the *Hokie Pok*ey to show off my team pride. My brother and his friend decided to be the University of Georgia Bulldogs and started yelling "Goooooo Dawgs … sick 'em!"

Our teams had a love-hate relationship. In the South, I grew up hearing that called "good old-fashioned hate." A true southern rivalry. Our friend's entire family were huge into the Bulldogs. When I say huge, I mean they were *HUGE* University of Georgia Bulldog fans. You know exactly what I'm talking about. Always running around yelling "Goooo Dawgs. Sick 'em. Woof Woof Woof." Fans who live and breathe for their teams no matter who they're around never shy about telling you stories about how their team always is in control, how they totally dominate every opponent on the face of the earth. I wanted to beat the Bulldogs so badly. *Gobble gobble gobble, Let's Go Hokies!*

As much as I was disappointed that my dad wasn't back yet to see how well my brother and I had mowed the lawn, I couldn't wait any longer to play.

I ran up and kicked the ball high and deep, almost into our neighbor's driveway. My brother came underneath the ball, catching it on the fly. We ran down the yard as fast as we could, and I tackled Jack deep in their own territory, the perfect start to the National Championship Super Bowl. My heart raced with competitive excitement. In my mind, I could hear the deafening roar of the crowd cheering us on for another great stop. The Bulldogs came up to the line for their first play. Jack leaned over to hike the ball as we crowded the line.

"Hut one, hut two." Jack snapped the ball and took off running deep, with me right on his hip. My teammate stayed at the line counting to five before rushing his little brother. He yelled "Five!" and rushed hard with his hands held high in the air to help block his opponent's view. Undaunted, the little brother threw the ball high and deep a second before his big brother could reach him.

Jack's eyes got huge. He smiled as he saw the pass coming his direction. I knew that look anywhere. I knew what was about to happen and I knew I could stop it from happening. As I spun around, I saw the ball about to drop into Jack's hands. I dove just in time to knock the ball down before he could get his hands on it. It felt so good to break up that play. I had just prevented my little brother from scoring a touchdown. My buddy and I celebrated like the Hokies had won the National Championship.

We eventually walked back toward the line of scrimmage. Just then, I noticed my dad and mom arriving back home. As they pulled up our steep driveway, I could see they looked upset. Was my dad angry about something with the lawn? I wish he could have seen it before we started playing. But it still looked good, I thought. What did he see that I didn't? There was no reason for him to be unhappy with me, was there? I became consumed by the look on Dad's face, worried about what I must have done.

My dad turned the car around to back into the garage. The old garage door rattled and creaked as it opened. The garage door going back down interrupted my worrying. When neither of them came outside to talk to us, I refocused on the game.

The Bulldogs came up to the ball; we got ready to stop them. As soon as Jack snapped the ball to his friend, I hopped up from my three-point stance, following up in his route. The quarterback threw a perfect pass that I couldn't catch up to, but I made it in time to hold Jack to a short gain. This was getting intense. Third down was coming up and there was a lot on the line. You should have seen the looks we were giving one another. Emotions were getting heated. Competition was fierce. No one wanted to lose. Bragging rights were at stake here.

Before third down could begin, the front door of the house squeaked loudly. We looked up to see my dad as he opened the door. A poorly timed interruption to the game. Once again, my dad looked so serious, not his usual smiling and joyful self.

"T, we need you to come inside for a moment. Boys, you can keep playing football until he gets back."

"Dad! Please, can it wait?"

"Now, T."

I pleaded with our friends and brother to wait until I got back to snap third down. I headed inside. What in the world was my dad so mad about? I had no idea what was about to happen, yet I already felt so out of control.

"Let's go sit down and talk in the kitchen with your mom." Dad's serious expression made me worry again.

I followed his instruction and walked into the kitchen where my mother was already sitting at the table. She looked like she had just lost someone dear to her. Who was it? What is happening here? I could not, for the life of me, imagine why they were both so serious and sad. And why only me? Jack helped with the lawn as well.

"Is everything okay?" I asked.

They looked at each other for what seemed like forever without saying a word. I was starting to think none of this had to do with landscaping. My dad finally broke the silence.

"Your mom and I have been meeting with several different specialists, trying to figure out what is going on with you at school. They have determined that you have dyslexia and focus issues, T. We are going to have to move you to another school . . ." Dad cleared his throat before he continued, ". . . and you will have to take third grade over again."

I couldn't believe my ears. My heart started racing and I suddenly felt sick to my stomach. This couldn't be real. I just passed the third grade; I shouldn't have to do it again. The last year was hard, but I got through it. *It is totally not fair to make me do it again!*

I don't remember much of anything else my parents said to me. Everything mixed together like a giant blur. Life as a kid was supposed to be carefree and fun. I should be out enjoying my summer break, crushing my brother and friends in football. Instead, I didn't feel like doing anything. Fear and anxiety stirred inside of me.

I could feel my eyes welling up with tears. "Please don't send me to a new school with none of my friends, Mommy and Daddy!" I began to beg. "Please, please! Please, don't make me repeat the third grade! It's not fair. I will do anything. I will work harder at reading. Please don't do this to me."

The look on their faces told me they were not going to change their minds, no matter what I said or did. I had no control over this scenario.

When I saw there was going to be no way out of this fate, I exploded with anger. "I will do whatever you say, but I won't love you anymore!"

I jumped up from the table and ran to my bedroom, slamming the door behind me. I threw myself on my bed, grabbed my pillow, and began to cry. There was no way I was going back outside to play football now. The National Championship Super Bowl didn't matter anymore.

I was wrecked. My young world was spinning out of control, and I couldn't stop it.

2

Not so Good Things

You made me; you created me. Now give me the sense to follow your commands. (Psalm 119:73, NLT)

AS THE LAST FEW WEEKS of the summer began to evaporate, I reluctantly accepted my fate, but not without exhibiting a bad attitude. Moving schools and repeating the third grade was far from ideal, so I diverted my attention to the secondary implications of the decision. I needed to be salty about all the things I was losing in order to eventually accept what was going to happen regardless.

To help me start walking a pathway of acceptance of this massive change in my young life, I started to focus on what I didn't like about my previous school. All in all, it was a great school. I had a lot of friends there. I have amazing memories of walking home after school with my buddies and playing in the creek, catching salamanders and crawfish. I loved to chase the girls with the crawfish. They were scared of the claws, and I enjoyed sending the girls into a panic. So, to help me not miss it so much, I focused on the not-so-good things about my previous school: no air conditioning, reading circles, and nasty old teachers.

I had been stuck with the one third-grade teacher every kid prayed they wouldn't get. She was the thing I most disliked about my old school. That teacher made my third-grade year at school downright miserable. In my eyes, she was a mean old witch who looked the part. She never smiled. She wore large, baggy dresses with a thin belt that she could quickly take off and use as a whip when needed (school was very different back then). Her old shoes made an eerie, almost sinister noise when she sauntered around the classroom. Magnified bifocal reading glasses hung from an old gray chain around her neck, with several little trinkets dangling off the chain. One for each student she had failed or locked in a dungeon somewhere, I imagined. Everyone seemed to be afraid of her, but I had an extra reason to be afraid: She made us read out loud. Third grade required more reading and a lot more individual reading aloud in front of the other students, which shook me and my confidence to my very core.

Every single time she called my name—no matter what the reason—I became full of fear. So much so, I struggled to do even the simplest things she asked me to do in class. I was an easily distracted kid to begin with. Any movement or sound, in or outside of the classroom, derailed me. So, adding in the anxiety of what this teacher was going to do to me made school a nightmare for me.

Reading time was pure torture. My heart would begin to race as soon as she started calling out the names of who was going to join her in the reading circle. I could feel my fear and anxiety increasing with each name she called to go to the back of the classroom. When

I heard, "TJ, please come and join us in the circle," my heart sank, and my hands got sweaty. I would stand up and slowly walk The Green Mile to my demise. When I joined the other kids in the circle, I noticed some of them looking just as scared as me. They were afraid of being called out to read for her as well. This gave me some relief that I wasn't alone in this situation, but there wasn't anything that was going to make me comfortable about being in the read-aloud circle. Inevitably, by the time I reached the small circle of wooden chairs, with no space in-between, only one seat would be available for me to choose from, and I would have to sit next to the grumpy teacher all the time.

The saving grace was that the reading circle took place in the back of the room, which meant only the kids sitting with me could hear me read or hear our teacher's negative comments. As we sat in this circle in the back of the classroom, taking turns reading out loud to her, she seemed to enjoy humiliating me for my nervous stuttering, skipping words, and extra choppy reading skills. I should probably say, "my non-reading skills" at the time. I was mortified every time she put me in this situation.

She would look down at me over her reading glasses with an evil smile and announce, "TJ, it's your turn to read for everybody." With a look of pure enjoyment, she would watch me and wait for me to mess up. "That's wrong, TJ. You are a bad reader. Maybe you are just stupid or retarded."

Her words stung me with so much hurt. The words "stupid" and "retarded" became tapes I played in my head constantly.

Every time, she forced me to continue, which only made me more anxious and more scared to continue. I had to keep pushing through—there was no way out of the torture of the reading circle. Seconds seemed like minutes as I desperately struggled to find my place again. My legs were straddled over each side of my chair, nervously shaking as if they were trying to keep up with my racing heart. Often, a classmate saved me by pointing to the place on the page where I had stopped.

I picked back up reading, messing up even more than before. She angrily interrupted me, "You can't read, TJ. Stop. Let your classmates show you how to read. Pay attention." I wanted to crawl into a hole and die, but there was nowhere for me to hide. To make matters even worse, I could hear some of my classmates snickering out loud and calling me "retard" under their breaths. (This is a terrible word and has thankfully become taboo. I only use it because it was my experience.) My skin felt like it was on fire with embarrassment and shame. My sweaty legs stuck to the hard wooden chair. I wanted to run away, as far as I could get, away from her and her harsh words. But I just sat there frozen in my chair, looking hopelessly down at my book. I was too ashamed to look up at any of my classmates. I felt like this world was not for me.

The world wasn't kind to dyslexic kids like me, as I would later be diagnosed. I have heard about other people who struggle with dyslexia who were instructed to crawl their way up to the front of the classroom before they read aloud to the class. It was supposed to help their brain work better so they could read better, but it only shamed them publicly. I didn't have to crawl through the classroom (thank God), but I believed I was never going to make it in this world.

On occasion, I hid from my friends after school. I waited for them to start walking home without me so they wouldn't see that my eyes were red from crying. When I got home, I tried to tell my mom about the horrible reading time, only to hear, "It's not that bad. You just have to work harder. Practice reading out loud to me more and you will be fine."

I wanted to please my parents, especially my dad, and even my grumpy old teacher to some extent, although I still can't understand why, so I started reading to my mom every night. I'd read aloud to her in the kitchen while she prepared our dinner. That was tough for me to do, especially while my brothers were running around playing. I was easily distracted by everything they did, making it hard for me to focus on what I was trying to read. I easily lost my place or drifted off, picturing myself eating eggs and bacon. My mind always seems to be doing weird, random things.

Even when I concentrated on focusing without any distractions, the letters on the pages sometimes literally moved around on me, appeared to be other words, or even disappeared altogether. When my teacher or my mom corrected my reading, pointing out words I had missed, I could then see the words correctly on the page. I got to the point where I made up sentences in an attempt to trick my mom into thinking I was reading better, not knowing that she had already read the book. Of course, she would call me out, causing me to only get more frustrated.

The more pressured or nervous I felt, the more trouble I had with the letters, the words on the page, and verbal instructions. Sometimes I could read the word correctly in my head, but then say the wrong word out loud. I became so frustrated, confused, and discouraged with my reading. To make things even worse for me, when our teacher gave us detailed verbal instructions to do an assignment or take a test, I couldn't track along with her because my mind wandered off, leading me to not follow her directions, do the task poorly, and get in trouble. I see now that my school was not equipped to understand how to teach students who learned differently.

Throughout my years in school, I got absolutely no pleasure in reading, only frustration. At the time, I understood two things for sure: reading was not for me, and it never would be. I also find it interesting and kind of ironic that I am now writing a book for others to read. I have struggled so much with the written word and reading, and now I am writing a book! The irony of this is not lost on me. I do now actually enjoy reading books, or should I say listening to audiobooks while reading along in a hard copy. How great is the invention of the audiobook on our smart phones? Whenever I have free time, I listen to a ton of audiobooks while following along in the books. Reading is still a challenge for me, but God has helped me overcome the anxiety of it so that I can continue to learn and grow.

Staying focused, however, has been an ongoing issue for me throughout my life. I struggle with focus to this very day. Just ask my family. My mind is often somewhere else when I should be focused on my wife or my children. They have become experts at noticing when something distracts my focus away and calling me out whenever I need it.

But as a third grader, I eventually figured out that it did not help to come home and complain about my frustrating day of reading out loud and being made fun of—so I started lying about it, saying I had a great day at school. To be clear, lying is not good, but becoming the kid who tried to only say good things about my days at school was a positive thing.

As for this first attempt at third grade, things got worse for me as the year went along. At some point, my parents started hearing from parents of other kids in my class who were also coming home scared and upset. Other classmates were scared that our teacher would start calling them names if they did not read perfectly. After talking to the principal and my teacher, my parents realized they needed to make a change for my sake. This started the whole journey toward what would be decided on the day of our National Championship Super Bowl.

My parents tried to figure out a new school for me to start in the fall while my brother stayed at our old school. They had found a school just a couple of miles away that specialized in learning issues, where I could be taught new and more efficient ways of learning. Unfortunately, after seeing my test results, the school officials informed my parents I was not a good fit for their program. It was too late for their intervention because I had already developed my own methods of coping, trying to overcome the problem in my own way. Control shows up in the weirdest places. Thus, my parents had to find yet another public school where I could repeat third grade. I would also be required to work after school with a specialist.

My parents' words kept going round and round in my head. "T, dyslexia is causing your eyes and brain to not work like other kids'. That's why you need to repeat third grade. You will have to do extra work at home to catch up, to improve your reading and comprehension skills." This devastated me. My world and my heart were rocked forever. What was the point? If I can't read, and nothing is able to change that.

I felt like a victim. I couldn't understand why God and my parents had given me this dyslexic thing. If God doesn't make junk, then why did He make me have dyslexia? If God truly loved me, why had He made me broken? I was miserable, scared of the unknown, and bitter. If they would just leave me alone, I was certain I would be fine. I didn't need to go to another school or catch up. I could read well enough to get by in life. I could understand street signs, names on packages, and even directions on food labels … just not books.

My parents started by having me work with an eye doctor to help me strengthen my eye and brain connections. Next, they added a therapist who specialized in learning issues to help me with word pronunciation, spelling, and comprehension.

Decades later, my mom shared with me that after about a year of her patiently working with me every day on physical therapy exercises for my eyes while I was repeating third grade, she noticed something very significant. Every night before she and my dad went to bed, they came into our rooms and kissed each one of us good night. One night as they came into my room, she noticed that my usual tightly clenched fists with white knuckles were now open and relaxed for the first time in over two years. All our hard work together was finally paying off in big ways. I was becoming less fearful, more relaxed, and more confident, and it first showed up while I slept.

What my mother didn't know was that I had been hiding a terrible secret, one I felt too much shame to confess. By making me come straight home after school and spending all evening working with her, my mother had rescued me from something way more painful than embarrassing reading circles. It would be many years before that dark truth was exposed. So, when my mother saw my relaxed body sound asleep, she could only see her little boy sleeping peacefully because of the progress we'd been making with my therapy.

Only now, as a parent myself, have I grown to fully appreciate and experience first-hand how that moment must have touched their hearts. It still touches my heart today. Just because we don't feel or see the results, that doesn't mean we're not improving or growing. Of course, I didn't have the ability to recognize this progress as a child. I just knew I had to work harder than anyone else.

This was all done for me at great sacrifice by my younger brothers and Mom. On school day afternoons when we got back home, my brother Jack was put in charge of watching our baby brother while my mom worked with me. I did not appreciate this at the time because I was an angry nine-year-old who could not play with his brothers or go outside like all the other kids having fun after school.

Most of all, I was angry at my parents because this was all their fault, not mine. Of course that's what I believed at the time. I blamed them for all my troubles. I turned inward and away from my parents. And God.

Even though my mother's dad was an Episcopal priest and we attended church every Sunday, I began doubting if there was even a God at all. I decided from that point on, I was going to take total control of my life and show everyone, including God if there was one, that they were wrong about me. At this time, the school system did not accommodate me, so I was forced to develop my own strategies to cope. I was going to work harder, longer, and do things "my own way."

I worked hard to always be in control of my world so I wouldn't be embarrassed at school anymore. I also tried to be funny to deflect the struggles I was encountering. When I messed up at school, I laughed at myself, making silly comments to distract others from pointing out my mistake. I would much rather kids laugh *with* me than laugh *at* me. I also learned to cope by smiling, while crying inside and putting up thick walls around my heart. I didn't allow anyone too close, especially teachers or my parents. I had to be in control from now on. My obsession with control had begun.

3

All About Me

"Ah, stubborn children," declares the Lord, "who carry out a plan, but not mine...." (Isaiah 30:1a, ESV)

BEING A BOY WITH SOME serious learning issues forced me at an early age to push through my struggles, which translated well to athletics. Thankfully for me, I had the opportunity to get involved in sports and extracurricular activities. Since school, and mostly reading, had torn me down, I turned to sports, music, and scouting to help build my self-esteem.

It didn't hurt that people noticed my athletic abilities in just about any sport I attempted. To get back at my parents for this "dyslexic thing" they had given me, I left football, basketball, and baseball to turn toward competitive swimming. Why swimming? It's simple; no one else in my family did it and I didn't have to rely on anyone else to win. The race was just between me and the clock. Swimming is a very honest sport from that standpoint. Plus, swimming cost a lot of money and it was all about me.

My parents did not want me labeled as "learning challenged" or stuck with the stigma of taking meds for my dyslexia and ADHD (Attention-deficit/hyperactivity disorder). Swimming helped me not get sucked into that label or stigma. More importantly, swimming helped me settle down and focus better. Since swimming is such a physically demanding sport, it helped my mind to slow down as well, enabling me to focus on my homework. At the same time, my parents also increased my protein and carbs. The extra nutrients not only helped my body to rebuild after tough workouts, but they gave my brain better fuel to develop and stay dialed in.

My swim coach, Coach Pete of the Atlanta Swim Association, was an amazing man with an even bigger heart. Our team motto was, "Swim Fast for Pete's Sake!" And I loved doing just that. Coach Pete was demanding, tolerated no playing around, in or out of the water, and practices were all business—no excuses. Two hours of intense, almost non-stop swimming left no time for talking or cutting up. Just enough time to literally catch your breath and get an earful from the coaches before you were off pulling through another set. I had to work hard to stay focused on what we were swimming, as well as keeping count, especially at the beginning of practice. The deeper I got into each practice, the more my mind slowed down and the better I could focus. Sometimes while swimming a long, hard set, my mind wandered off to think about food, especially doughnuts and milk. I pretended there were doughnuts at the end of each lane, so I swam faster to get there. Other times, I completely zoned out during sets by listening to the music playing over the pool speakers. One time, I zoned out in a swimming rhythm and kept on swimming past the completion of the set while everyone else took a break and watched me. I was too locked in to notice.

Coach Pete believed in me. I cannot overstate how he ignited a desire, as well as an ability, to succeed. He personally taught me how to channel my pent-up anger and energy to go faster in the pool. He also taught me with demonstrations that helped me visualize exactly what I needed to do. Combined with his verbal instruction, his visual guidance became a catalyst for understanding, both in the pool and in the classroom. I became bold, learning to ask for specific instructions that would help me understand.

He also built up my self-esteem and impressed on me that, in swimming, you get out of it what you put into it. The honest sport of swimming plays no favorites; the clock tells the truth. I loved having a level playing field. It was totally unlike what I experienced in most other places—especially in the classroom. Swimming didn't care if I struggled at reading or stuttered. All that mattered was how hard I worked and what kind of effort I put into swimming. As a result, I qualified to swim for the US National AAU swim team by the age of 14 as a breaststroke and freestyle sprinter. The next year, I won all my races, set personal records, and qualified to swim in my second Junior Olympics. My parents and brothers were proud of me and my efforts, and I was surviving, even doing better, at school.

Years later when my own kids were on their high school swimming team, I got the opportunity to coach opposite of Coach Pete, who was thankfully still coaching swimming after all those years. My daughter, Rachel, was in ninth grade, and on this particular day, she was struggling with her breaststroke. She lacked confidence about being able to swim fast enough to qualify for State. As she walked out of the locker room, looking sad and dejected, Coach Pete walked over to her. He gave her a big hug and had a short conversation with her. The next thing I saw was Rachel jumping into the diving pool to work on her stroke. After swimming several laps, she hopped out and gave Coach Pete a big wet hug. She ran over to me and shared how Coach Pete had helped her figure out how to swim faster, breaking down her swim into small blocks of time with a new strategy. She ended up swimming with a load of confidence and qualified for State. I still get emotional thinking about how Coach Pete blessed my daughter, just one of only-God-knows-how-many swimmers who have experienced an improved sense of identity because of their interactions with him. It's why I still coach high school swimming today. I want to help kids just like Coach Pete helped me and my own kids.

Swimming didn't always go smoothly for me, however. My need for control showed up in unexpected ways. In fact, in the end, my need for control cost me the sport.

The biggest race of my swimming career came when I competed in the 100-meter breaststroke at the Junior Olympics. I felt confident I could win this race. I had beaten my main competitor several times, and I was only getting faster each time I entered the pool. I swam my best race that day, but somehow my nemesis beat me by two-hundredths of a second. I had never lost in the breaststroke before. Sadly, I was not a happy loser or a good sport. I was so upset by this defeat that I decided to quit swimming immediately. I was done.

Anger was once again feeding my thirst for control, just as it had back in the third grade.

I chose to play football now that my swimming career was over. I always loved football. My dad was a good coach (not the team coach, but a coach just for me) and I loved spending time practicing with him. I started out as the place kicker for my high school team. At home, Dad had me kicking hundreds of field goals every day after practice as we waited for dinner. I had such an inner drive for perfection that I could stay focused in the game, just like I had stayed focused in the pool.

My drive for success paid off—I became the starting kicker and the backup tailback for the varsity football team in my freshman year.

During my formative high school years, my coaches, teachers, and my parents pushed me and supported me in profound ways. My music teacher told me, "T, your struggles and hard work now will be huge blessings in your life. You are a blessed young man. I will not let you settle or just get by." She was one example of many people who believed in me and held a high standard for my results. My parents came to every event my brothers and I participated in, on and off the football field. It felt so awesome to always have them there, cheering me on. I felt seen, valuable, and loved. I was determined to succeed and make my parents proud. My determination resulted in an extreme need to control the outcomes.

My dad was a good athlete himself. He was a former top-ranked tennis player in Florida. He loved all sports, though, especially football. He played for Virginia Tech, which has always had a good football program. He soon discovered that I had some of the same athletic talents, perfectionistic attitude, and a strong competitive spirit. Simply put, I did not want to be good—I wanted to be the best at everything I did. Sports, school, or life. Learning difficulties weren't going to slow me down.

My determination showed up in Boy Scouts as well when I decided I wanted to earn my Eagle Scout rank. I had started with Cub Scouts back when I was struggling in third grade. I loved the Boy Scout program and especially our troop, 298 at Northside United Methodist Church. So many amazing leaders and friends invested one-on-one time with me, teaching and encouraging me and keeping me accountable. I felt encouraged and had a chance of real success. Less than 4 percent of all Scouts ever earn their Eagle, the highest rank in scouting. I worked hard, persevering for nearly six years to become an Eagle Scout at the age of 14. This was a great accomplishment for me because of how challenging the rank is to earn. Plus, both my dad and grandfather were Eagle Scouts. So, it was not only a rite of passage, but an expectation for all the Sharitz boys. Both of my younger brothers earned the Eagle Scout rank as well, three for three.

Although I excelled in extracurricular activities during high school, reading aloud remained one of my greatest challenges. Dad racked his brain to find different ways he and I could connect, as well as help me to improve my stuttering, word pronunciation, and reading aloud in school. He had noticed that like him, I had a great love of music. Plus, I loved imitating radio announcers. He came up with the greatest solution: build a small recording studio in our basement.

When Dad pitched this idea to me, it didn't take me very long to jump at the opportunity. It required us working closely together, spending hours in his basement workshop working on the studio, just the two of us. We built several different electronic devices, including our first color television with an actual channel knob to change the channel and a wired remote control, which was high tech at the time. I learned so much from my dad about how to plan, organize, follow directions step-by-step, problem solve, solder circuits, and celebrate a job well done. One of the best things Dad taught me was to check off each task using different colored pencils. This amazing trick I would later apply as I took notes and studied in high school and college. The use of different colors to highlight words helped me to see the actual words and remember text content better, the best possible thing for me!

Finally, our simple studio was complete: two microphones hooked up to an audio mixer with inputs for my two turntables, a dual cassette deck, and a reel-to-reel tape recorder. I know this sounds completely archaic today, but in the late '70s and early '80s, it was awesome. All this equipment helped me immensely to overcome my reading and speaking issues. I recorded myself reading out loud as I practiced being a radio disc-jockey. When I read too fast or messed up, I stopped the recording and redid it till I got it perfect. This routine also helped me discover a love and passion for mixing and editing music. Plus, I got to do this with my dad. All of this was extremely significant for me.

One of my best friends from high school, Tommy Sullivan, lived behind us and shared my love of music and radio broadcasting. We spent countless hours together, recording each other reading and pretending we were disc jockeys on the radio. Little did we know that all this fun and creative practice would lead both of us to one day work professionally in radio and television.

Tommy became the "Quixie Quacker," the station mascot and on-air personality for WQXI and 94-Q in Atlanta. That might not mean much to others, but it was a big deal in our neck of the woods. As a matter of fact, Tom Sullivan's legendary broadcasting career became the real-life inspiration for many of the DJ antics on *WKRP in Cincinnati*. To show what a great guy Tommy is, he was so grateful for the mentoring and practice that my dad gave him in our little basement studio that he paid it forward to other aspiring radio announcers. One such aspiring announcer was a passionate local high school senior named Ryan Seacrest. Yep, the same Ryan Seacrest that is on every other television show these days including *American Idol*. After mentoring Ryan, Tommy placed him on the air for the very first time on Labor Day weekend in September of 1992 at Star94 FM in Atlanta. And the rest, as they say, is history.

Looking back now, it's easy for me to see how God orchestrated people coming into my life with the purpose of encouraging, sculpting, and molding me into the young man He planned for me to become. My dad, Coach Pete, my Scout leaders, and Tommy were all crucial men in my life. The lessons they taught me were truly invaluable.

But I did not realize any of this at the time. I had overcome dyslexia and ADHD to become a passionate, driven, and self-focused individual. Sadly, I was only focused on what TJ wanted and needed to do to be successful. To control. I had no time for serving others or God—it was all about me. I thought I was in total control of everything. In a nutshell, I was starting to become a control freak.

4

Real Deal

The heart of man plans his way, but the Lord establishes his steps. (Proverbs 16:9, ESV)

AFTER LEAVING THE SWIM TEAM, I excelled in football, soccer, and track during high school, earning varsity letters in football and track all four years. I became a high school All American football player and a track sprinter with different Division 1 scholarship opportunities for college. Some Atlanta newspapers even compared me to OJ Simpson, "The Juice." We did have the same jersey number: #32. They'd call me the "real deal" and "better than just OJ" *(Really!)*. "Ridgeview High School has their very own juice, not just OJ, but a V-8" and "TJ stands for Tomato Juice."

Being raised in a Virginia Tech family meant Virginia Tech was the only college I wanted to attend, just like my dad and grandfather. My paternal grandfather was a graduate of Virginia Polytechnic Institute (VPI) class of 1932. (Virginia Tech was known as VPI back in the day.)

Grandfather TJ Sharitz worked as an Agricultural Extension agent until being drafted to serve our country in World War II. Killed while serving, my grandfather is buried along with some 10,500 American war dead in Lorraine American Cemetery in Lorraine, France, near the German border. It's the largest US Military cemetery in Europe.

So, my father grew up most of his life without a dad. As a young man, my dad was a true rascal, much like me—not following others but leading and chasing his dream of a college education. He was able to attend Virginia Polytechnic Institute because, before he died, his father had made arrangements with his former boss, Harry S. Sanders, one of three VA Tech professors who started Future Farmers of America back in 1927. Mr. Sanders promised my grandfather that if anything were to happen to him during the war, he and his wife, Julia, would see to it that my dad, Charlie, would be raised as a gentleman with integrity and character, and would get a college education at VPI. The Sanders honored that, loaning my dad $2,000 interest free to pay for his education.

Dad worked hard after graduating from VPI to pay back "Mom and Pop" Sanders (what he lovingly called them) for college. Once my dad had paid them back, he calculated how much interest would have accrued and sent them another check. Weeks later, my dad got a very nice thank you letter from them with his check. They appreciated the gesture, but that was not what they had promised TJ. Thus, my dad took that money and funded a scholarship in Harry Sanders' name. Today that scholarship helps students studying AG Science.

Nearly every year, our family spent Thanksgiving with Mom and Pop Sanders at their home in Blacksburg, Virginia. During one Thanksgiving dinner when I was about ten years old, I asked Mom Sanders, "Mom, when I grow up and come to VPI, will you make me sugar cookies and take care of me like you did for my dad?"

Everyone broke out in laughter.

"Well, you've first got to get into VPI. However most likely I won't be here," Mom Sanders said.

Unfortunately, by the time I graduated from high school, I did not have the grades I needed to be accepted at VPI, now Virginia Tech, even with my dad's connections and involvement at Tech. Also, based on my academic performance during high school, my parents had reservations about me being able to handle the level of work at Tech, which they kept to themselves. It also didn't help that my high school counselors busted my chops, telling me "You are just a jock. College level work isn't for you. Maybe a trade school, but definitely not a college like Virginia Tech. If you were somehow able to get into VA Tech, you would most likely flunk out and have to move back home." *How's that for encouragement?* Actually, their doubts in my abilities fueled my fire to want to prove them wrong.

I took control of my situation and accepted a football athletic scholarship to a two-year junior college in Banner Elk, North Carolina. This junior college was known for helping athletes improve their academics before heading on to their Division I colleges. My plan was to attend classes, play football, and do well academically, of course, so I could transfer to Virginia Tech on a football scholarship. I set my sights on the goal of being a place kicker, convinced that would give me the highest chance of success at playing football with the Hokies. Of course, this was only my intermediate goal—I was convinced I was going to make my way into the NFL. A kid's dream come true.

Banner Elk was beautiful with hemlocks and evergreen trees everywhere. Awe-inspiring mountains surrounded the town. It never seemed to be overcast there except when it snowed. It was a beautiful place to attend college, play football, and while I was at it, further my radio broadcasting career. What little free time I had, I spent working at the college radio station. The professors at the junior college were great, and the classes were small, with lots of extra support whenever I needed it.

My experience on the football field, however, was filled with bad days. I'd been recruited as a kicker and tailback, but once I got there, I wasn't allowed to kick or run the ball. Instead, they decided to switch me to a defensive back. There were several DBs already, so this didn't make any sense to me. The coaches gave no explanation; they just tossed me out there.

The day before our first game, the coaches made us fight amongst ourselves to see who the four starters would be. Literally fight each other. The last four men standing would get to play. Fortunately for me, I injured my shoulder at practice before the melee began. When they realized I was too injured to fight, the coaches decided to redshirt me (sit me out for the entire year so I could play two more years there). I had lost control over my football future. This frustrated me beyond repair.

As the end of the semester approached, I called my dad. "If you love me, Dad, you will get me transferred to Virginia Tech for the spring semester. I can't stay and survive in this atmosphere."

I don't know how he did it, but I was finally accepted into Virginia

Tech as a transfer student. It helped that I had made all As, earning a 4.0 academically in junior college, but I suspect Dad must have pulled some strings as well.

My first day on VA Tech's campus, I stood with my dad, looking out over the massive drill field, war memorial, and classroom buildings. He said to me, "T, you can do this. There have been students walk across this drill field and eventually graduate from Tech who were not as smart or as determined as you. It will take everything you've got to succeed here. You will graduate from here. Your mom and I believe in you, and we love you." I tried not to let Dad see the tears in my eyes. Tough football players don't cry. Integrity and character were everything to my dad. He believed those qualities defined you as a man. It made me proud to know he believed in me.

I was also blessed to have Mom Sanders still alive and living in Blacksburg while I attended VA Tech. I visited her regularly during my years at Tech. I think Mom Sanders loved my weekly visits as well, especially while I was taking Basic Floral Design class during my senior year. I dreamed of owning my own advertising and video production company, so I took this class to help me learn about design, meet girls, and, yes, get an easy A. Every week I took Mom Sanders a flower arrangement from class, and in return I got her time, unfiltered wisdom, and more than my share of her famous sugar cookies.

Because both the past VA Tech coaches and the new coaching staff had recruited me, once I was enrolled at Tech, I was finally given the opportunity to fulfill my childhood dream. I got to play football for the Hokies. I had succeeded in doing what no one thought I could do. All I needed to do was stay focused, finish strong, and graduate.

I made memories on and off the football field, enough to last a lifetime. On game days, after our pre-game meals, we got to meet different alumni and former players. One Saturday, I noticed an elderly man staring at me with a great deal of emotion.

I walked over to the man, and he asked me, "Are you TJ Sharitz's grandson?"

"Yes sir, I am. My name is Thorold Joseph and I go by TJ. My dad, Charlie, is TJ's only son, also a graduate of Tech, class of '58."

He smiled. "Your grandfather and I were bunkmates and best friends in college. You look and smile just like he did."

I knew then without any doubt—God is one amazing orchestrator. This incredible moment was put into play long before my dad or I were even born. I knew I was exactly where I needed to be.

5

Change of Plans

A man's steps are from the Lord; how then can man understand his way? (Proverbs 20:24, ESV)

IT IS AN HONOR TO be named after my grandfather, but Thorold Joseph is clearly not the name I use around town. Most everyone knows me as either TJ, Dad, Dad 2.0, Coach Sharitz, Meathead to special family members, or Mr. Chapstick to my Passion City production team. My favorite nickname, however, is from my wife Jaci. *Pooh.* Only she can call me that.

Interestingly, I thrived academically at Virginia Tech. I majored in communication studies with a concentration in broadcast and film production, as well as graphic design. My classes challenged my learning disabilities, but my interest in what I was learning motivated me to overcome the difficulties. Plus, everything I pursued had a hands-on aspect to it. Running a film or video camera, sitting down at a video editor or at a mixing board, allowed me to be creative. Things always made sense to me in this space. I could easily understand how things worked when I was creating something with my hands or using video or audio tape.

During my sophomore year, I created and produced a radio sports interview show called "The Tech Connection" from my dorm room turned studio. I interviewed different teammates about the upcoming games, injuries, preparation, family. It was easy for me to do with my past radio experience, and I was on the field with them every single day. The guys jumped at the opportunity to be on the Connection or any radio show. The show aired on Saturday mornings before every kickoff. I loved doing this show. It grew in popularity so much that the Tech Sports Network took over the show the following year. This allowed me to move into shooting, and later directing, the Head Coach's Sunday morning game recap television show.

Athletically, however, things at Tech didn't work out exactly the way I had so carefully planned and envisioned. I was a good place kicker and punter. I would drill 50-yard field goals with consistent accuracy. My punt average was 45+ yards, with 4.7 to 4.9 second hang times. That's the amount of time the ball stays up in the air. The greater the hang time, the more time the team punting the ball has to go down the field and cover or tackle the punt receiver with little to no return.

I brought that same energy that I had as a third grader playing in my front yard to practices at Tech. My special teams coach knew I was also a 200- and 400-meter sprinter. He strongly suggested that I run slow if I wanted to kick. But I was a control freak, all about me and doing my best and nothing less than 100 percent. I had learned to give maximum effort, especially when someone said I couldn't do something. I had to prove myself, so I ran my best during our sprints. I ended up being one of the fastest on the team, behind two Olympic sprinters and a super-talented and tall wide receiver."

As a result, I never got the opportunity to actually kick for the Hokies.

Kicker was the position I wanted to play. Our new head coach did not want a kicker who was five foot, eleven inches (listed as six foot), 225 pounds, and ran a 4.4 in the 40-yard dash. I was simply too fast to be a kicker. Should have listened to my coach and run slow.

Today I realize this is all part of my control issues. I struggle to let someone else define or seemingly limit me. But that's not what my coach was attempting to do. He saw potential in me, but I was too stubborn and prideful to accept it or follow his advice. I played those positions well, but I wasn't determined to succeed as anything other than a kicker. I would stick around for hours after practice, kicking and shagging balls all by myself. I figured at some point, our head coach would see persistence and make the right decision, but I was wrong. He never did.

Time for me to take control. I would become a kicker, no matter what it took.

Through one of my former college teammates who was now playing in the NFL, I found an agent to represent me. While my agent looked for opportunities for me, I went all in on making my kicking dream a reality, kicking every day when the team wasn't practicing and imagining myself as a USFL and NFL kicker and punter. Before long, my agent helped secure me a couple opportunities to try out with teams in the new USFL league. Unfortunately, I couldn't land a spot on any of the USFL teams. However, those tryouts ended up being great preparation for the day when my agent called with exciting news. He had secured me the tryout of my dreams. I'd been scheduled for an open tryout with the New York Giants.

I was so excited that my lifelong plan and all my extra work was finally about to pay off. I packed my bags and kicking cleats and drovc up north to where the Giants held their training camp. When I arrived, I felt I had truly arrived in life. I was on the field with some absolute studs, most of whom would become Super Bowl champions within a few years.

Despite being absolutely starstruck and speechless, this moment did not intimidate me in the least. I somehow felt like I belonged. No one knew me or the challenges I had experienced. Plus, this experience was not tied to classwork. If I could pull this off, I could focus all my energy, which I had been using to overcome all sorts of previously mentioned problems, toward football. I was ready to overcome this challenge and win a spot on the roster.

My plan was in motion. But I couldn't control it.

A few days into summer training camp, I was talking myself up with several of the guys, which reflected my confidence. I suppose my cockiness deserved to be checked.

And it was.

During a simple warmup drill, the placeholder pulled the ball up right as I started my kicking motion so I would slip and fall, looking like the rookie I was. When I saw him start to pull the ball away, I stopped my kick. My knee on my plant leg didn't like that sudden change and immediately buckled. I fell to the ground in extreme pain. The sudden stopping motion on my leg had injured my knee.

Playing football for so many years as a running back, delivering and taking hits, I had never been hurt like this. Yet here, I tore my knee without any contact from another player or even the football. How does that even happen? My NFL kicking career was literally over before it ever began.

My coaches let me know that the odds of me ever kicking in the NFL after hurting my knee were slim to none. Every season there were always more great kickers just waiting for an opportunity. There wasn't a good enough reason for a team to take a chance on someone who has a compromised knee.

I was so discouraged and confused. This was not my plan. In fact, I had no other plans—this was what I was going to do with my life. I just knew I was destined to be an NFL kicker.

My lifelong dream had apparently come to an end. I was crushed. I felt so out of control. I could not accept this reality. God gave me this desire and ability, didn't He? I convinced myself that He wanted this, and only this, in my life. Of course, I was not spending much, if any, time in prayer, trying to understand what God actually had planned for me. I felt like I had to just grit my way through and simply acknowledge Him occasionally along the way. I suppose I had taken God on a ride. My ride.

More than one of my coaches tried to encourage me to look at the bigger picture. "Unlike a lot of the players who only have football for their livelihood, you have earned a college degree. You clearly have potential of success in anything you put your mind to."

They made some great points. My coaches clearly cared about my well-being as a person, not just a player. I also knew how competitive the kicker market was and how replaceable players were. However, there was just no way I could walk away. I was so close to my dream; I wasn't about to give up now.

So, I moved to Miami in the fall of 1983 to rehab my knee, and to support myself I began working for a concrete restoration company. There were specialists down there that the team highly recommended. Besides, the upcoming winter months were going to be too miserable in New York if I were to stay up there. South Beach seemed like a nicer "comeback trail" to me.

Many other NFL prospects had all come to the rehab center on the campus of the University of Miami, each of us working our way back to accomplish our dreams of playing in the NFL. I had never felt so known and understood before! We pushed each other to not give up and to try harder. I think everyone knew that the odds were against us. Maybe 25 percent of us would get another shot, which means even fewer of us would make it into the NFL. There is so much competition to get signed by a professional football team. A commonly used phrase in the league is "next man up." It's a great statement of desire and preparation, meaning that everyone should be ready to seamlessly replace the injured player in front of you. Unfortunately, that means some people are the "last man down" and can easily be forgotten about and moved on from. I looked around at these men and resolved that I was going to beat the odds. I was determined to become the next man up before anyone else.

Rehab was insanely demanding. I fought my body to overcome what it thought it could not do. My therapist constantly yelled at me to push through the pain, to keep my form in whatever exercise I was doing. On the occasions we were in the ocean, taking advantage of the geographical benefits, I felt more optimistic about whatever drill we were working through. There were many nights, however, I felt like I needed to give up. But I couldn't. I wouldn't.

This is where I would love to tell you this great comeback story. About how I got called up by the Giants just as the 1986 playoffs were starting because their kicker had an ingrown toenail and would have to be sidelined for a week. In that one start, I nailed a desperation 62-yard field goal at the end of regulation to win the game and push us deeper into the playoffs. That other kicker got healthy, but I was the hot foot, so they kept me on until we won the Super Bowl. Oh, and I kicked a record nine field goals, the only points in the game. Final score: 27-20 against the Chiefs. It would go down in history!

I will save you the effort of Googling what happened. I never made it back to the league. I gave it my very best shot, but I couldn't land a spot anywhere.

What is funny about all of this is how I had taken control and determined what I was going to accomplish, yet when it didn't work out, guess who got the blame? Not me. I once again blamed God. I was mad that He didn't see my plan through. It was a really good plan. He pulled the ball away from me, letting me kick high into the air and having me fall right on my proverbial backside. God "Lucy'ed" me.

In the old *Peanuts* cartoon, Lucy was so cruel. She never let Charlie Brown kick the ball, always pulling it away just before he kicked. Aaugh! *Peanuts* author, Charles Schulz, was once asked why he never let Charlie Brown kick the ball. His response fits all too well with my story, "You can't create humor out of happiness." At the time, I did not find this rookie hazing in the least bit funny, as I lay on the grass doing my best Charlie Brown imitation. My knee hurt so bad and there was nothing I could do about it. It felt so unfair. Looking back now, I can see how my plan wasn't God's plan for me. God used this timeless cartoon stunt to redirect my path.

6

Mic Drop

O my God, in you I trust; let me not be put to shame;
let not my enemies exult over me. (Psalm 25:2, ESV)

I CLEARLY HAD TO COME UP with a new plan for my life in a fairly quick manner. Since football was out, my college degree was in. I searched various local newspapers for any job opportunities in broadcasting or advertising.

This was way before the internet or cell phone, so the only way to find these gigs was through the printed newspapers job ads and a few trade publications. After several months without any luck, I was able to track down an old Key Club faculty advisor I had met back in high school. Bill Edwards worked in Savannah, Georgia, as the sports director and anchor at WJCL-TV 22. After we caught up, he said my timing was perfect for a new job.

His television station had just finished up the last interviews for the only open reporter's position. Bill promised he would put in a good word for me with the news director if I could send him a demo of my work right away. The only problem was I had no real-world broadcasting camera work to offer as a demo. The only samples I had were various short films and sports shows I shot and produced while at Virginia Tech, and I had no quick access to these.

Bill stressed to me that I had to act quickly on this because the news director had already narrowed the candidates down to a former Miss Georgia, and they were about to make her an offer the next day. I tried to explain to him that I had no experience on camera, but that didn't seem to deter him. Taking control, I ended up promising him I would come up with something that day to overnight to the station.

I had no video camera, cell phone, GoPro, or computer that would allow me to shoot, edit, and send a demo. I turned to the Miami Yellow Pages to try to find a place or person who could help me. Yellow Pages have become relics, but then they were my best choice, and I poured over the printed list of area businesses and their phone numbers. I felt overwhelmed and doomed. I needed to improvise quickly.

At last, I found a small video production studio close by that said they could help me out. I rented a camera, microphone, desk, and a chair from them and attempted to recreate a newsroom. I wrote several different fake news story scripts, just like I had done in my basement with Tommy years earlier. I then recited these scripts on camera to show the news director my on-camera appeal, along with my writing skills. Once we finished recording, I convinced the studio to let me use their editing equipment so the news director could see my editing skills as well I sent the tape off just as I promised.

Somehow, I beat out Miss Georgia for the position as the new medical reporter, cameraman, and editor. Please let me be completely transparent here. I did not get this job because I had a great demo (it was honestly pretty bad), but because I showed creativity in overcoming obstacles. Plus, my friend Bill promised management I was worth the huge risk. In my mind, I had taken back control of my life.

Looking back, I now know that God was in control because I didn't do anything special to deserve this job. God tried to get me to see that He had always been there for me, this time by inserting Bill into my life years earlier for just this moment. But I didn't want to admit that to myself back then. The thought that I solved the problem through my own creativity blinded me to seeing God's orchestration.

On my first day in the WJCL newsroom, I received a news car (an old station wagon but I didn't care) and an assignment for the newscast that evening. Ready to show the world my talents and creativity, I got my first assignment—take a camera package and go shoot interviews, B-roll (extra footage of stuff related to the story), write a script, and then edit it all into a two-minute package to be aired during the six o'clock news that day. Lucky for me, I had learned to use similar cameras in college, so I needed very little help to get going.

I got the interviews done, shot some great B-roll, and headed back to the station. The news director showed me to my desk where he handed me the forms to write my script. He told me I needed to turn in the script before I left for lunch. He promised to have his revisions ready for me on my desk when I got back. I sat down and eagerly typed out my script with excitement and great confidence. My dyslexia fears couldn't outweigh the momentum I felt at the time. Besides, I had figured out how to get A's in my advanced broadcast writing classes, so this should be just fine. Once I finished, I dropped my script off in his box and left for lunch, knowing I had just written an Emmy Award-winning story. I had crushed my first assignment.

To celebrate, I treated myself to some amazing Savannah seafood for lunch. When I returned to the station I walked in with a strut of accomplishment. I went over to my desk to review what little tweaks the news director had made. Much to my surprise, I didn't see a script on my desk, so I walked into the news director's office to ask him about my revised script. He told me to look closer, because he definitely made his edits and placed his approved script on my desk. I walked back over to find a tiny piece of paper that I had overlooked. It had one word on it, "The." I turned back with confusion about this revision. He said, "That's a great start, now finish it up," then walked back into his office. I stood there feeling like an idiot. Okay, I admit my writing skills could use some work, but only one correct word? Talk about being humbled. I was instantly transported back to third grade, I felt so ashamed of myself for my lack of competence.

I eventually got a script approved and moved on to the editing phase, something I felt more confident about, but I was so shaken from my boss's critique that I wasn't about to take anything for granted. That evening, my first story aired. Seeing it on television for the first time gave me great relief. I resolved to take more time and be more careful in the future.

I later learned that my boss played that same one-word prank on every new reporter who came in. He had no idea I was dyslexic. In fact, he had liked the first script I turned in. I took it in stride, but I felt the need to work extremely hard to hide my secret issue from him and everyone else.

As a TV news reporter at WJCL, I spent the next eight months asking lots of questions, soaking up all the techniques and wisdom I could from my co-workers.

Before long, I became the guy everyone wanted shooting and editing their stories for air. But no one asked for assistance in writing. Perhaps they wanted to retain control of that for themselves, but it still bothered me. I worried people had figured out my shortcoming.

One morning, the news director asked me to go cover a special Kiwanis Club meeting featuring a well-known educational specialist. I was pumped because Kiwanis held their meetings at a wonderful local seafood restaurant, and free seafood was my all-time favorite food. After lunch, I set up my camera and began recording. As she began speaking, I found myself surprised to hear her talking about issues with kids who have dyslexia.

The education specialist went on and on about how horrible dyslexia was, calling it a learning "disability." My ears perked up, and I listened intently to what she was saying. She went on to add that the best way to help these children was to protect them from their weaknesses and struggles, telling the Kiwanis Club men in the audience that no one should ever push or encourage these kids with this kind of learning disabilities into a situation or profession that would expose their limitations. I could not believe my ears. Was she honestly saying this about me?

It's funny that in that moment I didn't feel angry or even upset. Nor did I want to dunk her into the lobster tank, though that would have been funny. Instead, I felt myself getting calmer and more at peace. Why would she be saying things that weren't true? As she continued, she even went as far as to say that if a dyslexic student made it into college, they should never be allowed to do activities like sports because that would take too much time away from studying for them to succeed in earning a degree. Come on, *really*? I know a lot of dyslexic student athletes who graduated from college. Some even tested to have higher IQs than their peers. This had better be a joke or reverse psychology because this lady's speech reflected the exact opposite of everything I had experienced and done. For me, hearing negative comments, people trying to label me as disabled or not good enough, only fueled my desire to succeed, to prove them wrong.

When she finished speaking, she opened the floor up for questions. I found the courage to ask her with great peace and clarity: "Please let me be sure I understand what you are saying. Are you saying that if a student has a learning disability like dyslexia, stutters, or simply has trouble reading, you strongly discourage them from ever playing football in college or getting a job as a radio announcer or television reporter?"

"Absolutely correct. That would just be too much pressure for them. They would ultimately fail with this disability. Even dyslexic adults cannot cope under a lot of pressure like that."

I smiled and said, "Hello, my name is TJ Sharitz. I am a reporter and cameraman for WJCL TV-22. I am dyslexic. I have a learning difference, not a learning disability. I learn differently. I worked hard to improve both my reading and comprehension, and to correct my stuttering by pretending to be a radio announcer reading out loud. I graduated from Virginia Tech with a degree in broadcasting and a minor in graphic design, all while playing football for the Hokies."

Mic Drop.

After that mic drop moment, you could have heard a pin drop in that banquet room. She finally broke the silence, acknowledging my success and noted that I was the exception, not the rule, because not all kids end up like me. As she explained her argument, she slowly moved her position away from an imperative and finally told me that she would be looking at dyslexia through a different lens from that day on.

How I responded to her words felt like such a God moment for me, something I could have never imaged or coordinated. I knew in that moment, I helped prevent this speaker, a woman considered an education specialist, from giving another shortsighted speech about learning "disabilities." I also knew that many of the fathers in that room that day were there to get specific understanding of how to guide their dyslexic children. It felt good to give them my perspective, some personal insight on how to raise their own little third-grade TJs to become productive, successful, and most importantly, unashamed adults.

What I didn't know at the time, was that God wasn't the only one involved in this serendipitous moment. (I might have used Siri to help me with that word. I've come a long way, but I don't think anyone can spell that correctly by themselves). My boss had figured out about my dyslexia. He sent me to this specific Kiwanis meeting with the purpose of creating an impactful story about overcoming impossible challenges. He definitely got what he was hoping for. I might not have won an Emmy for that story, but I am certain I helped a lot of people out there know what is possible.

It's obvious that God gave me the peace and words from my heart so that I didn't destroy that opportunity by spewing my old bottled-up pain. Speaking up to the education specialist also gave me some unique courage in other parts of my life. For instance, I tracked down Miss Georgia and asked her out to lunch. We had a really great time and she shared that she was not mad by my swooping in at the last minute and stealing her job.

7

Bold Enough

Hope deferred makes the heart sick, but a longing fulfilled is a tree of life. (Proverbs 13:12, NIV)

A FEW MONTHS AFTER MY DYSLEXIA news story aired, I came into work to find a note on my desk. The general manager wanted to see me right away. I walked over to his office where his receptionist ushered me in. She closed the door behind her as she walked out. I had been called into the "principal's office," awaiting whatever bad news only he could deliver. It felt like I was in trouble, only I had no idea what for. My self-talk turned negative and full of self-doubt.

The GM walked in, pretending not to notice how much I was sweating. He quickly broke my tension by telling me he had good news for me. He had received a call from a producer who ran a show called NOVA. Since it launched in 1974, NOVA had become the most-watched prime time science series on American television, reaching an average of three million viewers weekly on PBS. Getting a call from NOVA was a big deal. It would be a big jump for me career-wise.

While vacationing in Savannah with his family, the NOVA producer watched various local newscasts over a two-week period. He had been impressed with several of my various medical stories, especially with my camera work. He wanted to talk with me about coming to work for him as a freelance cameraman and editor. My GM encouraged me to consider the offer. He told me this was a great opportunity for me to showcase my skills; plus, they wanted me to move to Atlanta, he said, which is a major television market. He went so far as to say I could be done at the station that very day, just to ensure this opportunity wouldn't slip through my hands. Besides, he had several people lined up wanting a position like mine. I instantly recommended that Miss Georgia take my spot.

As soon as I walked out of the GM's office, I called the NOVA producer. He asked me a few questions to make sure I had actually shot and edited the stories he had seen. After a few minutes, he offered me $300 a day as a freelancer. Unfortunately, the offer didn't include benefits or guaranteed hours. The show was not produced in Atlanta, and I would be responsible for any stories based in the southeast, which would not happen every day. But still, I would be making more working one day a week for NOVA than I did working 40-50 hours every week in Savannah. I could not turn this down—I said yes immediately. The producer promised me a feature the very next week.

I was so excited about what had just transpired, I had to call someone. I called my dad at work. He agreed I had made a good decision, but he advised me to downplay the part-time and inconsistent part of the story when I told my mom. It probably was a good idea to not worry her. My dad also offered to let me move back in until I got some money saved up to move back out on my own. This gig checked all the boxes for me. I felt like I had arrived.

The following Monday morning I drove down to the NOVA studios to meet my producer and get started on my new job. I sat in the lobby for what seemed like forever before he came out to greet me. He finally appeared and thanked me for coming in but said it with little enthusiasm. I immediately knew he was about to give me some bad news. I could tell he didn't know how to segue into what he needed to tell me, and finally he just ripped the band-aid off. His crew had been filming the Scream Machine roller coaster at Six Flags of Georgia over the weekend, and they didn't secure the mounting of the cameras properly. The cameras didn't survive the fall. Therefore, the budget he had to spend on employing a regular freelancer had to be reallocated toward replacing the cameras.

Wow. This opportunity was over before it began, just like my experience with the NFL.

Okay, what was God doing here?

In one of my favorite books, *The 4:8 Principle: The Secret to a Joy-Filled Life*, Tommy Newberry states "By the grace of God, each moment is a new beginning, a new dawn for your potential."[1] This was that moment.

I briefly considered going back to Savannah, but I quickly dismissed that idea. Besides, Miss Georgia had already taken my spot as the new reporter for WJCL. I decided to seize this moment, to take advantage of being in one of the biggest television markets in the country. I needed to find work in Atlanta.

A few months earlier, an engineer I had worked with in Savannah had made the move to CBS Sports in Atlanta. I jumped in my car and headed straight over to their studios to see him. I walked into the lobby, explained my bad fortune to the receptionist, and asked if my former colleague was in the building. Sadly, I could only remember his first name. She smiled and said she knew who I was talking about, and yes, he was on site that day. She dialed his extension and explained that I was in the lobby hoping to speak with him. She smiled back at me. He would be right out.

After a few minutes, the engineer walked into the lobby. He greeted me with a big smile and a hug. I was so glad he remembered me and at least pretended to be excited to see me. I began to tell him what had just happened with NOVA. He laughed, saying that kind of thing happens a lot in this business, and he asked me what he could do to help. I asked if he knew of any openings or anyone I could talk to about working as a freelance cameraman or video editor. He said they possibly had an opening and walked me down the hallway to meet the operations manager. My friend introduced me as one of the best cameramen and editors he had ever worked with. That was maybe a little bit of a stretch, but I was certainly thankful for the shoutout.

The manager asked if I had any samples of my work. Thankfully, I had a demo of my work from WJCL in case anyone at NOVA wanted to see it. It felt good to not have to scramble this time. He fed my video into a tape machine so we could watch it on twenty screens and one super large monitor in his control room. I nervously stood beside him as he watched the entire eight-minute demo without saying a word or showing any emotion. This was intimidating, especially since I had no idea what to do next if this guy didn't find

my work acceptable. He shuttled the demo back to a couple di
spots, asking me technical questions to see if I really did shoot the footage. He smiled, even laughed, as I explained some of the crazy, outside-the-box shooting techniques I had come up with.

We walked over to an editing bay with equipment that was newer, nicer, and more advanced than what I had been using in Savannah. He asked me to jump on the machine and edit a short voice-over (VO). I slammed together the VO faster than I would normally do; I wanted to impress him with my speed.

Probably risky to choose speed at the risk of quality, but it made sense to me at the time. I hit play on the finished product and before it was finished running, he smiled and asked me, "How soon can you start?" I jumped up. "I'm ready to start right this minute, sir." He shook my hand. "Welcome to the broadcast production team."

I thought I had it all under control. I went to Atlanta to work for NOVA and ended up working for CBS Sports and WAGA-TV 5 instead.

For the rest of the day, I learned to operate different cameras for both film and video at the studios before I headed home to tell my parents what happened. They were so excited for me, exclaiming how greatly God provided for me on this day of need.

I wasn't so willing to say that God was the one who coordinated everything. It was clearly my brilliant idea to go see my friend (even if I didn't know his last name) and be bold enough to ask for a job. But I didn't fight my parents on this fact. I kept the reality of me being in control a secret, but in my heart I knew the truth. I did not yield control.

8

Determined Pursuit

You have captivated my ... heart with one glance of your eyes .... (Song of Solomon 4:9, ESV)

WORKING AT CBS WAS AN amazing gig for me. I couldn't imagine NOVA being anything as good as what I stumbled into. Every day seemed to have something new and exciting to offer. I was fortunate to spend years traveling the country working as an on-field cameraman in some of the most iconic college and professional stadiums. I also got to shoot and edit thousands of stories for CBS's various sports and news programming. I even covered the "Rattlesnake Roundup" (yes, this is a real event).

I am absolutely terrified of snakes. It was awful. After talking to the event director, we decided I would set my camera on record while he and other contestants walked it around, placing my camera at various snake dens. All the while I sat in the safety of the truck. My plan might get me fired, but I didn't care. I'm that scared of snakes, especially those with fangs. Thanks to the director and competitors who moved my camera around, getting close-up snake strike shots, the footage was awesome, albeit horrific and frightening to edit. Ironically, I ended up winning a regional award for "my" creative work.

One day, my good friend and fellow cameraman, Gregg, came into my editing suite with a rush of enthusiasm. "Hey man, you've got to come meet my girlfriend and her super-hot best friend. They're in the commissary right now waiting for me to get off work." Why not? I was single and always ready to mingle with beautiful ladies.

We walked over to the commissary where he introduced me to his stunning girlfriend, an anchor/reporter in Peoria, Illinois. He then introduced me to her friend Jaci. Gregg's girlfriend jumped in, saying they needed to hurry up for their double date, with Gregg's roommate serving as Jaci's date for the night. I was already seeing someone at that time, but I remember feeling dejected that I wasn't the fourth member of the night's festivities.

A few months later, I got into a big argument with the girl I had been seeing regularly. During the argument, I blurted out, "We fight like an old married couple." She misinterpreted what I said and thought I just proposed.

"Yes, I will!"

Wait a minute. You will what? I didn't just ask her to marry me; I was criticizing her. The next thing I know we're engaged. I had no idea how we got to that point. More importantly, I didn't know how to get out of it. This so-called "proposal" hadn't gone at all the way I had always pictured proposing. However, I liked the attention of being engaged, and I was scared of the fallout, so I just went along with it. Talk about giving up control. What was I doing?

After a few months, things went from bad to worse. I finally had to tell her our relationship was over.

The next day at work, I asked my buddy Gregg about that girl he introduced me to the previous year. Did she end up dating the guy she went on that double date with? Then I shared all about how I pulled the plug on a terrible engagement. He felt bad for me and gave me Jaci's number. That's a good friend right there.

I was so excited to call Jaci that I wasn't even nervous. I dialed the phone and a lady with a very strong southern accent answered. She informed me that "Ms. Jacqueline is no longer living here." She apparently had moved back home to save money for graduate school. This nice lady gave me Jaci's parents' phone number, which I immediately called. I wasn't nervous until her father answered, "Hello, Bieberstein residence."

Gulp. "Hello. May I speak with Jaci?"

"Who may I say is calling?"

"My name is TJ Sharitz. I am one of her friends."

His response was unexpected. "Hello TJ, I am her father, John, and I know all her friends. You, sir, are not one of them. Do you have any more lies for me?"

Where do I go from here?

"Okay, you are right, sir. We aren't friends exactly. I met Jaci last year at CBS Sports, where I work. She came in with one of her girlfriends named Donna who is dating one of my good friends and fellow co-worker."

"Donna who?"

Oh, come on! I have a hard enough time remembering people's first names. I was sweating and couldn't think straight. I knew her last name, but my mind went blank. Before I could come up with an answer, he asked me, "Why are you calling Jaci a year after meeting her? Are you now desperate?"

Another gulp.

"No sir. I was in a relationship when I met her, and now I am not."

There was a pause, and then he asked me, "So you are one of those good-looking guys on TV?"

"Well sir, I'm not in front of the camera anymore. I am a cameraman and video editor."

"Oh, so you're not good looking. Why are you calling my daughter?"

I could tell he was thoroughly enjoying this back-and-forth banter. I wasn't. I gulped down some confidence and said, "I just wanted to ask her out for lunch."

As he started to reply, I had a God moment. I interrupted him, "Donna's last name is Schulte! Donna Schulte."

He replied, "Well, if you know her, you can call her here tomorrow morning and speak directly to her. But if she agrees to meet you for lunch, you are buying."

"Yes sir. And thank you sir."

Somehow, I had survived the most intense phone interrogation ever and had been granted permission to call Jaci the next morning. I wondered if all this was worth it for just a date, but I couldn't stop now. When I called back in the morning, Jaci answered. She had no idea who I was, nor did she remember ever meeting me. Fortunately, she did remember coming to CBS with Donna and meeting a lot of different people, so my story seemed plausible. Somehow, I convinced her I wasn't a serial killer, just a nice guy who wanted to take her to lunch, no strings attached. She agreed to meet me the following day for lunch in a small cafe.

The next day, I arrived at the cafe early. I hoped I could recognize Jaci. This was before cell phones, Facebook, or the internet, and it had been a year since I had briefly met her, so I wasn't sure I remembered what she looked like. Then I saw a single young lady walking down the long-stepped walkway alongside a cascading stream. As she passed the waterfall, my eyes bulged out of my head like a cartoon character in love. This girl was flat beautiful, stunning to see. She had a short spiky haircut, was wearing an amazing strapless cocktail dress with painted fruit, and hot red high heels. Next thing I knew, God spoke to me, "You are going to marry that beautiful young lady." *Really God. Now you show up? I don't have time for this beautiful lady. I'm here to meet Jaci.* I did secretly hope God was right and that this young lady was Jaci. I couldn't tell. Plus, *I'm in control here, God. Thank you, anyway.*

I held my breath as the beautiful young woman came to my table. It was Jaci. *Thank you, Jesus.* I should listen to God more often. He was right.

While sharing a nice lunch we discovered we shared a lot of similar interests, hobbies, and dating morals. Then she dropped a bomb on me! She said she wasn't interested in dating anyone—including me—right now or in the near future because she was headed back to Auburn in Alabama for grad school in a few months. *What?* I needed to take control. At the end of our time together, Jaci agreed to hang out with me again on Friday night, just two days later, after I got off work. Not technically a date.

Friday morning, I called Jaci to confirm our plans for later that evening. She answered the phone before her dad did (*thank you, Lord*). As I started to share my idea for us that night, she stopped me in my tracks.

"I can't go out with you tonight. Something has come up."

Are you kidding me? I defeatedly replied, "That's okay, you don't have to explain, I totally get it."

Jaci sensed my disappointment and said, "You don't understand. We just found out that my dad has cancer. I want to stay home and spend time with my parents."

A few minutes later, I called her back, asking for their address so I could drop off a little something for them. I promised I wouldn't stay. She kindly gave me their address, and I quickly started making a fresh batch of pralines with walnuts. I drove over to their house that afternoon. When I rang the doorbell, Jaci answered the door. She invited me in to meet her mom, and of course, her dad, the "interrogator."

The four of us ended up sitting at the kitchen table talking for hours as we got to know each other. We even shared dinner together. I learned that her dad, John, was a former United States Air Force pilot, like my dad. He had flown jet fighters and became a captain flight instructor. When he left the Air Force, he continued flying as a commercial pilot for Eastern Airlines. My dad, on the other hand, after leaving the USAF, became an engineer and purchased his own airplane with two former Air Force buddies. My dad loved flying all over the country. I have great respect for all those who are serving, and those who have and how they have sacrificed to protect our families and freedoms. It helped to have these conversations with John and break down my fear of him.

The time spent around Jaci's kitchen table felt so comfortable. I think I could have stayed there even longer than I did, although we hung out for over 12 hours together—I finally left there around three in the morning! It wasn't the date I was expecting, but it was way better than whatever I would have planned for that night.

Again, I heard that little voice in my head saying, "You are going to marry this girl." *What am I supposed to do with that information? Not like I can tell them.* Why did God continue to plant seeds of marriage, and to this girl who had already proclaimed she was not going to date anyone. *Come on, God, really?*

Still, I drove away thinking to myself, *What an amazing family she has. I am going to be so lucky to join their family.*

Over the next couple of months, I pursued Jaci with every means necessary to spend as much time with her as possible before she headed to Auburn in January. On my way to work, I took her lunches almost every day when she was working at the pharmacy. Sometimes, I sat outside of the pharmacy and just watched her work because she was too busy for a break (*it's not as creepy as it sounds*). Seeing her always made me feel lighter. I was totally in love. Of course, I couldn't tell her that because it would totally go against her original proclamation of not dating anyone, and it was way too soon in the relationship.

My friends all told me that I had lost my mind over this girl, that I'd lost all control. They wanted me to date other girls who wanted to date me back. What sane single guy turns down dates with other young ladies for a girl who lets you sit by yourself while watching her work? How is that even dating? No hugs or even a kiss goodbye. But I felt deep in my heart that "she was the one." God told me so.

After the new year, Jaci left for graduate school in Auburn as planned. I visited her often, and even though we weren't officially dating, clearly our relationship was continuing to grow.

Whenever I was in Atlanta, I spent time getting to know her parents better. I snuck ice cream to her dad when he was in the hospital for his cancer treatments. I wanted to help in any way I could, so I did a lot of yard work for John (yes, I made a beautiful lawn that would be perfect for a football game if the occasion ever arrived).

When my parents met Jaci, she won them over immediately, especially my dad. He enjoyed her spending hours with him discussing football. She acted like his daughter, and he loved that.

Once Jaci's dad was out of the hospital and feeling better, he introduced me to his favorite breakfast establishment, the Waffle House. I know this makes no sense to anyone from the South, but I had never been to a Waffle House. I didn't realize what an institution it was to Southerners. Of course, he used these meals together to interrogate me further and learn more about my intentions with his youngest daughter.

Several months later, as we sat at the Waffle House eating our All-Star breakfasts with smothered hash browns, both my feet shook as I built the courage to say to him, "John, I want you to know that I love Jaci very much. My number one priority is helping her finish grad school since that is so important to her. I would like your permission and blessing to ask her to marry me."

John smiled and said, "Yes, I will gladly give you both my permission and blessing to get married. Good luck, T."

I couldn't believe I had won over Jaci's father! After the first conversation eight months earlier, when I lied to him about being Jaci's friend and he had interrogated me, I thought there would be no possible way I would ever get his blessing to date his daughter, let alone marry her. Now I just had to convince the girl I "wasn't" dating to go along with it as well. That was one thing that felt totally out of my control.

9

Beginnings and Endings

"I am the Alpha and the Omega, the First and the Last, the Beginning and the End." (Revelation 22:13, NIV)

ON A HOT SUMMER DAY in 1987, Jaci and I joined her parents on their houseboat on Lake Lanier. *This is the day!* I nervously scrubbed the hull of the boat while Jaci helped her parents prepare lunch to take on board. Once they got everything ready topside, we headed out for a small island with a beach just outside the harbor. John got the boat into position and tied up, and Jaci and I jumped into the lake to cool off.

Jaci's mom, Mary, tossed a raft float for Jaci to lie on and I swam over to her. The two of us floated in the lake's cool water, talking about how nice it was to get away from school and work. I told her how much I had enjoyed getting to know her family over the past several months and how great I felt our "friendship" was.

Then I grabbed her hand and blurted out, "Jacquelyn Marie Bieberstein, will you marry me?"

Jaci looked at me with a puzzled look, "Are you serious?"

"Yes." I replied.

She told me if I was serious, I should get down on one knee to propose. I began to drift down below the surface, down a few feet to the bottom of the lake. I wasn't sure how long to stay there, but popped up at some point and repeated the question.

"Jacquelyn Marie Bieberstein, will you marry me?"

This time, with a gigantic smile, she said, "Yes!" Then she leaned over and kissed me. She turned and yelled at her parents, who were still on the houseboat, "I think I just got engaged!" They looked genuinely excited, and I was relieved that this engagement went better than the last one.

Did we ever have conversations before we married about what being a couple of faith would look like? No, we did not. Did we ever discuss what following Christ would look like in our life together? When we started dating, I told Jaci I was a Christian. She knew I believed in God, and that was enough for her. I think I gained a few extra points by telling her my grandfather was an Episcopal priest and that I was an altar boy. Jaci had been raised in the Lutheran Church; I was raised in the Episcopal Church; so, we knew our faith upbringings were similar: Go to church every Sunday, say your prayers at night—the Lord's prayer with God Bless Mom, Dad, sister, etc.

We got married on February 11, 1989, in Jaci's family church in Stone Mountain, Georgia. I was 29 and Jaci was 27. She wore her mom's altered wedding dress and was stunningly beautiful as she walked down the aisle. Neither of us were too nervous. I didn't even mess up my vows. For a dyslexic with ADHD, this was a pretty big deal!

We got an apartment just east of Atlanta. As newlyweds, we enjoyed all the time we had together despite both of us still having busy schedules. Jaci worked at a local pharmacy and drove down to Auburn to work on completing her master's in pharmacy care systems. I left my job at CBS to work at Firearms Training Systems (FATS) as their video producer and director. FATS made training simulators for firearms safety that were like giant video games. They used real weapons fitted with special lasers hooked up to air tanks to simulate actual live fire. Soldiers or police-in-training interacted with a large screen in front of them, shooting the bad guys when they came into view. It was a cool and important job as it helped first responders be better prepared for whatever scenario they could encounter. I had no idea when I took the job with FATS how valuable that experience would be later in my life. I thought I was taking control by switching jobs, but there is no way I could have known what lay ahead of me and how it all fit together.

When the Fourth of July holiday came around, we needed a break, so Jaci and I drove up to my parents' mountain cabin in Big Canoe, close to Jasper, Georgia, for a few days. The four of us played at the lake beach and rockslide spillway my dad had designed years earlier.

On the third of July, my mom and Jaci dropped me off at the tennis center so I could play a few games with my dad. He had just played two hours of doubles in the 100-degree heat and was enjoying a water and cigarette break when I arrived. Excited to see me, he yelled that he was warmed up and ready to beat me easily.

I twirled my racket in hand and said, "Let's go, Meathead!"

I spent the next hour and a half running from one side of the court to the other, while my dad worked me over, gloating about how easy this was.

"Can't you just shut your mouth, old man, and play?" I shouted at him. He had the biggest smile on his face as he pummeled me.

That evening, back at the cabin, my dad asked Jaci to come over and sit with him and talk. She told him she would only come join him if he put out his cigarette. He did, and she went to sit with him. They shared a few stories and laughed endlessly. I wanted to come over and join them, but it felt like a special moment for the two of them. In typical fashion, my dad said something sarcastic, "Sitting here with such a beautiful young lady will probably kill me, but at least I'll die a happy man." She thought that was cute and told him how much she loved him, but also how much she wanted him to quit smoking.

That next day, we packed up and headed back to our apartment so Jaci could finish up a few things at the pharmacy before she had to head down to Auburn. It was a bummer to leave on the Fourth of July, but we'd spent a great few days with my parents. We headed back home refreshed.

My parents also headed back to Atlanta that day because my dad wanted to go to a show at a local comedy club that night. They stopped at his office on the way home so he and Mom could process payroll for his staff. He called me from his office asking, almost begging, that we come along that evening for the comedy show. The whole family would be there, including my brothers with their girlfriends. I hated telling him no because it sounded like fun, and he was so insistent that we needed to come. I told him I was sorry to let him down, but I promised Jaci I would drive her down to Auburn that night so she could be fully focused on jumping back into school. When my dad realized he wasn't going to be able to convince us, he said, "We'll really miss y'all and I love you both. Bye, T." I remember how that moment stopped me. *My dad hardly ever told me he loved me.* I knew that he did, but he didn't say it very much. I really appreciated hearing it.

Not long after I hung up the phone, it rang again, but this time it was my uncle calling. Somehow, I knew something was up with my dad.

"What's wrong with Dad?"

With sadness in his voice, my uncle informed me that my dad had just suffered a massive heart attack. He told me how Dad had been working at his desk with a cigarette in one hand and a freshly poured whiskey in the other when he suffered the heart attack. My dad was pronounced dead shortly after arriving at the hospital.

When we arrived, my mom was so apologetic for not being able to save my dad. She had done everything she could to try to revive him on the floor of his office before the paramedics arrived. I assured her it wasn't her fault and that it was only fitting that he passed away on the Fourth of July. As a former United States Air Force pilot and patriot, July 4 was his favorite holiday.

My dad was my hero. I always wanted to make him proud, ever since learning how to perfectly manicure a lawn as a boy. We loved spending time together. He was a ton of fun, the true "life of the party," and a great dad. Maybe most significantly to me, he had built an amazing relationship with his daughter-in-law. Dad was only 52 when he went home.

While all that seemed incredibly meaningful to me, I also felt suddenly out of control. I assumed I had everything figured out in my life, and then with no notice whatsoever, I realized I needed my dad now more than ever. I needed more time with him, for him to meet our future children. I needed to be able to call him up and ask him whatever random question I was stumped on. I had so much more I needed to learn from him. There was no safety net anymore … it was all up to me.

My heart was crushed. Even with Jaci by my side, I felt alone and lost without him. I became bitter and angry with God. "You keep messing up my life, Lord! Just leave me alone. I always do better when I am in control. You keep messing things up."

I lived in a season of bitterness with God for a long time. I could not reconcile the decisions He was making and how it affected me negatively. My glass was half empty now without my dad.

I would think about how Paul claimed that *for those who love God, He makes sure all things work together for our good.* (Romans 8:28) I tangibly thought it was a gigantic load of garbage. There was nothing good about any of this. There was no conceivable way I could accept this loss as something good. I was so mad, and I felt like nothing was going to pull me out of the pit I found myself in.

The following year, Jaci and I were expecting our first child. We made the special announcement to my family when we all gathered for my brother Bobby's wedding. Everyone was so happy for us, but Dad should have been there in his groomsmen suit, crying with excitement. As much as things were going well for us now, I was haunted with anger about what seemed unfair.

A couple of months later, I was downtown editing a video project for work when I got a call from Jaci. While she was at work at the pharmacy, she noticed blood spotting and called her doctor. He reassured her not to worry as this was a common thing. His advice was to go home and rest in bed. I told Jaci this seemed like a good idea and that I would wrap up everything quickly and head home to join her. Neither of us were too concerned because she had recently had a good doctor's visit and was now 14 weeks along.

However, instead of leaving right away, I got hyper focused on editing clips of tactical situations for an upcoming firearms training. Jaci called me a few hours later. She felt weird, she said, and was getting scared. I dropped everything immediately and drove home as fast as I could.

When I arrived at our apartment complex, I found Jaci lying on the steps. Deciding she could not wait any longer for me to arrive, she had desperately tried to pull herself up the stairwell to the parking lot. She had to get to the hospital. Our Rottweiler, Katie, was sitting right beside Jaci, protecting my pregnant, scared wife as she lay on the steps. I rushed to put Katie back in the apartment, then helped Jaci to my car. I sped to the hospital with much regret for not coming home sooner.

About halfway there, Jaci told me I could slow down.

That didn't make any sense to me, so I sped up.

"I lost the baby, T."

I couldn't comprehend how she would know and insisted we could get there quickly, but she told me that she felt the baby go. No need to hurry anymore.

We made it to the hospital where we got the official news. We lost our baby. A boy. We named him Michael Joseph Sharitz. I was absolutely crushed.

I felt so much guilt. I had let down Jaci and this defenseless little baby, choosing work over family. If I had left work when Jaci first called, I was convinced everything would have been okay. Jaci blamed herself for losing Michael. We were both hurting and brokenhearted. All of this felt like too much to handle.

First, my dad, and now our child?

I lost a lot of my joy after my dad died in July, then the loss of our baby took what joy I had left. I concluded that if God is in control, He must really hate me. I was beginning to think the feeling was mutual.

10

Out of Control

Unless the LORD builds the house, its builders labor in vain. Unless the LORD watches over the city, the watchmen stand guard in vain. (Psalm 127:1, NIV)

FOLLOWING THE LOSS OF OUR infant son, we were able to get into a medical study at Emory University that was based on determining the causes of miscarriages. This probably extended our grief some, but we wanted to figure out if we were going to experience the same thing if Jaci got pregnant again. We learned that our baby had a chromosomal abnormality that always leads to failed pregnancies. In their findings, we were told that everything was normal with us individually; the miscarriage was just "one of those fluky things." This seemed to reinforce the conclusion that God wasn't concerned about our good. He could have stopped this from happening, but He didn't.

The only tiny bit of comfort I could find was that Dad was in heaven and would welcome Michael as his first grandson. My mom suggested, "Charlie is such a stinker. He's up there in heaven and gets the first grandchild all to himself with none of the work."

So true, but where again was God in these painful losses? I felt like God had abandoned me and I was all alone. I felt more broken than ever. It was me against the world again. This world was not working for me.

I had no control over life or death. I knew that. But what I could control was my own pleasure. To lessen the pain, I allowed myself to take solace in looking at pornography, a familiar activity that went back to my younger years. Growing up, my two younger brothers and I would often sneak into my parents' room to look at my dad's *Playboy* magazines that he kept hidden in his dresser. We were fascinated by the beautiful naked girls on the pages … what boy wouldn't be? It seemed okay and just part of being a boy. But porn was my first giant step towards control, and at the same time to prove to myself I was not gay, which I clearly was not.

Over the next several years, Jaci and I tried to get pregnant again, including nearly four years of infertility work. "Lovemaking" became clinical, not fun or intimate. Spontaneity and romance were gone, replaced by hormone cycles, scientific tests, and temperature windows. Nothing was sacred. Intercourse was replaced by speculums, test tubes, and sperm specimen cups. As anyone who has gone through infertility treatments knows, it is a very humbling experience for couples. It also became evident to us that conceiving a child wasn't just science, because numerous times, the science added up to us being pregnant, yet there were no positive results. We needed God to bless us. There were some things that were out of my control, no matter how hard I wanted things to be different.

To keep us sane during the years of the aggressive infertility regiment, we slowly developed a good sense of humor about it. Even my brothers and Jaci's sister "offered" to help us out, poking fun at me and my obviously weak swimmers. On top of that, since I was having trouble getting his daughter pregnant, my father-in-law John also jumped in with advice, suggesting I wear baseball hats turned a certain way, not wear blue jeans or boxer shorts, etc. He enjoyed teasing me, often calling to offer his own suggestions. He even went as far as offering to come over and coach me. Just for the record, that never happened.

To add to our stress levels, we bought our first home with some extra financial help from my Uncle Jack. This is always a stressful thing to navigate, but we stretched ourselves even more by choosing a home that couldn't be considered a "starter home." We wanted to buy a house where we could stay for the long run and raise our future children.

Future children. To acquire that goal, I focused on "doing" … while my sweet wife became more focused on seeking help from God in prayer. One night as we were lying in bed she asked me, "Do you pray for God to bless us with children? Because I do." Did I pray? At the time I thought it was kind of mean for God to put it on her heart to be a mother if it wasn't going to happen. But yes, I suppose I did pray, but we never prayed together.

Shortly after getting settled down in our new digs, I lost my job at the firearms training place (FATS). Of course, I did! Why would anything good happen to me? I had no indication my job was in jeopardy. If I had known, we wouldn't have bought that house.

It was a great home, but we were extremely house poor with only one income. So poor that Jaci's parents would buy groceries, drive them over to her work, and put them in her car. Without that love and support, we would've starved to death or at least lost our new home. Jaci prayed a lot, but not me. Not anymore. I was harboring bitterness and anger towards God.

Jaci knew I was desperate to control something, so she recommended I open my own video production company. *Wow, she believes in me!* That was all I needed.

Well, she might say it differently. She would probably say something more like I'm kind of a "my way or the highway" type of guy, that I couldn't make concessions to work within the constraints of a big company. She would most likely add that I wanted to do business my way because I believed it was the *right* way. But this is my book so I'm sticking with her believing in me, which I'm sure is true too.

I didn't seek any wisdom from God's Word or pray at all about it; I just took the bull by the horns and did it. I hated the idea of working for someone else, and freelance jobs were hard to find. I had no business opening my own company, but I knew I could work hard enough to make it happen. Since I had no money available to help with startup costs, Jaci's parents stepped in and loaned me the money I needed, interest free just like Pop Sanders had done for my dad's college education. They also loaned me their personal computer so I could launch Sharitz Productions.

The same determination and work ethic that helped me overcome learning struggles came in handy with my new video production business. As the months went by, I picked up several small projects, creating some momentum for growth. At the same time, I slowly began to reflect on how my early childhood struggles and hard work ethic might have been a blessing after all. Was this God's plan all along, or was this just a result of my control and hard work? I didn't know.

Since these first videos would become the foundation of my business, Jaci and I agreed that every dollar given by a client would go into their project—I eliminated any profit margin to overdeliver on the job as promised. Clients were thrilled with the end products. But the model of business wasn't sustainable forever. I needed to start making money to get back on my feet.

One of our friends who had left a big advertising agency decided to team up with me to pitch a new business relationship I had been cultivating for months. The potential client was a local health club chain that wanted to run a big TV commercial campaign. We didn't have much of a chance of landing this big account, but we gave it our best shot. We ended up getting this account which gave us financial stability and led to more new business. Eventually, we became the health club chain's agency of record and could tout this client to other prospective clients. I finally started making money … and lots of it. I was able to pay back Jaci's parents, clear off our other debts, and even start putting away money for retirement. I was becoming very pleased with the kind of results I produced when I took control of things.

With things going so well with the business, it was time to set up an official business bank account. I went down to meet with an old family friend named Nancy. She was a bank manager and had helped me open my very first checking account when I was 12 years old. She had known my dad very well, and it made me feel proud to present her with a large deposit to start a new account. As I sat down in Nancy's office at the bank, she told me how exciting this was for her to be able to help me with the start of my new business. She had done the same with my dad many years prior when he started his own engineering and parking consulting business. We reminisced about him as she completed some of the banking paperwork.

Then Nancy asked me to go to the lobby to grab a blank deposit slip. I jumped right up from my chair and eagerly dashed toward the lobby, when suddenly, a strange smell hit me. *Gun oil?* Why in the world would I be smelling gun oil inside the bank? From that moment on, everything moved in slow motion.

Being midmorning, the bank lobby was relatively empty. I saw two older people standing at the counters conducting their individual bank business, two employees helping them from behind the counter, and two other banking employees at their desks in the open lobby area. Then I noticed three men in long, black trench coats and wool caps walking toward the counter. I watched as each man slowly pulled his cap down over his face. The smallest of the men had a long scar on his cheek. I then spotted another man dressed exactly like the other three. He stood adjacent from me by the doorway to Nancy's office.

My heart was pounding out of my chest. Because everything appeared to be in slow motion, I started to consider putting my old martial arts training to good use. I thought about grabbing his gun and forcing the other would-be robbers to their knees, but there were other customers in the bank and I couldn't risk getting them hurt or killed in the event something went wrong with my plan. I turned to the lookout man and made direct eye contact with him. I firmly asked, "May I help you?"

With that one question, the slow-motion effect ended. The guy crammed his sawed-off shotgun into my face directly underneath my nose. "Get back in that office and sit down, or I will blow your [blank] head off!"

I backed up and turned around to go back to sit across from Nancy's desk. The lookout guy kept his gun barrel firmly on the back of my head.

"Nancy," I called out as calmly as I could. "We have a problem."

Without looking up, Nancy replied, "Do we not have the deposit slips out there?" She looked down and opened her drawer and said as she looked up, "I forgot I have some right here in my top drawer." In an instant, I saw her face turn bright red with an expression of disbelief and fear. This was not a dream or a drill, but a real and potentially deadly situation. Nancy instinctively reached her right hand to try to trigger the alarm underneath the top of her desk.

"Lady," the lookout man yelled at her. "Unless you want to wear this man's brains all over your dress, you'd better not touch the [blank] alarm. Just sit there with your hands on your desk and don't move."

We sat there silently for what seemed like 20 or 30 minutes. It was actually less than three. I sat with the gun barrel still firmly pressed against my temple. I was doing everything I could to slow down my racing mind and stay focused on sitting still. This is a very difficult thing to do with attention deficit issues, even under the best of circumstances. I could see the man's face in the reflection on the glass covering the picture on the wall behind Nancy's head. I focused on studying his facial features, as he apparently had forgotten to pull down his ski mask to hide his face.

My mind started racing at hyper speed; I would miss my business celebration dinner with Jaci, but I would get to see my dad in heaven if this goes south. I tried to reassure myself that I was jumping to the worse possible conclusion.

The next thing I knew, the gun was off my head. The robbers left in a hurry with a lot of cash. Thankfully, I had brought in a check instead of cash for my deposit or I would have lost it all). Nancy jumped up and ran to lock the front doors. She announced that we were in total lockdown, instructing everyone in the bank to sit down and wait for the authorities to arrive. I found a blank sheet of paper and a pencil and used it to begin drawing the facial features of the evil man who held me captive. I also wrote down the physical descriptions of the other robbers and what details I could remember about everything, including the gun that had been pressed against my head.

Local police arrived quickly. Several detectives started interviewing each of us. A female detective sat down with me and I immediately shared my crude sketches and descriptions of everything I recalled. I described specifically the shotgun that had been crammed up against my face.

She looked at me with a skeptical expression and firmly asked, "How can you stay so calm and together after experiencing such a life-threatening ordeal? Did you know this was going to happen? Were you the lookout that got left behind?"

Are you kidding me? Was she seriously accusing me of being a part of this robbery?

A large, well-dressed man entered the bank and came directly over to where I was now being interrogated. As she continued drilling me with questions, exploring theories of how I must have had something to do with this robbery, the man spoke up.

"Detective, why don't you ask Mr. Sharitz who he used to work for and why he knows so much about the weapon used in this robbery?"

I looked up and realized this man was one of the FBI directors I had worked with when I was producing "shoot-no-shoot" training scenarios for my former employer, FATS. He had helped my crew produce several life-threatening scenarios for training his agents. One such scenario was a bank robbery. The detective instantly backed off and took my notes to help with her investigation.

I may have appeared calm to the detective, but this event shook me. I honestly regretted not acting when I had the opportunity. I know things ended up fine because no one was hurt, but it felt like such an out-of-control few minutes. I did not like it at all, but I was glad all my effort to overcome dyslexia and ADHD came in handy in that situation, even if it made me look like a suspect. I had learned how to deal with a lot of pressure and created ways to slow things down in my mind whenever I felt stressed. Despite this ability, I let everything play out with a real chance of disaster. Some would say that God was in control on that day, but that's not where my head and heart were. At the time I couldn't see how my past and present had come full circle. Was God showing His loving control by preparing me for this encounter in advance? I simply couldn't see it at the time because I wasn't trusting Him to be in control; I just failed to assert control when I had the opportunity. I needed to be better next time.

It would take months before I felt the full impact of this event. How could I be so fortunate to have survived this bank robbery? Had God protected me from harm? If so, what was His plan for me now?

11

Nothing if Not Persistent

See, I am doing a new thing! Now it springs up; do you not perceive it? I am making a way in the wilderness and streams in the wasteland. (Isaiah 43:19, NIV)

WITH LIFE NOW GOING BETTER for me professionally, I figured I could begin to splurge on some things for our home. Jaci and I were both tired of the cold, clinical processes we were going through to try to get pregnant. In fact, we had stopped all that craziness and started doing things the old-fashioned way. We began working out weekly, getting massages, and best of all we spent actual time loving each other. I decided it would be a great idea to buy a spa hot tub for us to enjoy together. I had it installed on the back deck, surrounded by woods and with plenty of privacy.

One day after work, I created a special evening for Jaci and me. I put a bottle of champagne on ice, created a platter of chocolate covered strawberries, and turned on some music for us to enjoy the *hot tub life*. I hoped to put romance and excitement back into our love life now that we weren't taking temperatures, charting cycles, and taking medicines to improve our chances.

When Jaci got home, she had such a strange response to the environment I had created. She wasn't mad, but she wasn't excited either.

"Welcome home, honey, come join me. It's time to have some fun."

"I can't get in the hot tub."

"Sure you can! Hop on in!"

"I really can't, TJ."

"Come on, sweetie. The water is just right, not too hot."

She grabbed my hand and lovingly looked into my eyes, saying, "T, you are not listening to me. I cannot get in the hot tub."

"What! Are you kidding me? Are you trying to tell me you're pregnant?"

With a huge smile and a hug, she replied, "Yes, we are actually pregnant!"

I lost my mind with excitement about this news. I couldn't believe it was real. As much as I wanted to picture Jaci holding our baby—I just knew she was going to be a fantastic mom—I was afraid to hope for this reality. The disappointment had become too much. If this was true for me, I know it was very true for Jaci. She wanted to be a mom so badly. How could I control the outcome? Somehow, I knew I couldn't.

During this time, my video production company had grown into a small advertising agency with a few employees. Without any marketing plan or real effort on my part, we kept winning new clients who wanted our services on all kinds of advertising and video production projects. Mix in my type-A, workaholic personality, and the business began to generate lots of income and land even bigger opportunities.

I sought to hire people who could compliment my skills and keep me away from things I wasn't as strong at. One hire was a talented and creative graphic designer. She had just finished working as an intern at a successful casual Tex-Mex restaurant chain. She talked me into reaching out to her former boss to win their business. Like us, her boss had just announced she was pregnant with their first child and was a little overwhelmed. I had never worked with a franchised restaurant chain before, so it felt like a stretch, but I thought it was worth the effort since I had a referral in my pocket. I called the director of marketing, Cari, and left a voicemail indicating that her former intern thought we would be a great fit to work together to create some local marketing programs for the franchisee's stores.

I expected to get a call back from Cari, but she never responded. I left voicemails with her every few months—for nearly two years. I wanted to set up a meeting, knowing I could land their business if I could just talk to her. At some point, I knew these messages would be annoying to her, but I am nothing if not persistent. I needed to land this account and I wasn't going to give up. And as it turned out, I was right to keep trying.

On December 30, 1994, Jaci went into labor, and we rushed to the hospital. As the hours went on, things got more and more tense. With every push Jaci made, the baby's heart rate became more stressed. Finally, at 3:30 in the afternoon our daughter arrived—without a sound. While inside the womb, she had somehow wrapped the umbilical cord around her neck twice. She couldn't breathe due to the cord being coiled so tightly around her neck at the time of delivery. The nurses snapped into action with what could only be described as a frantic confidence. They placed the mask over her tiny face and with one squeeze of the airbag, we saw her turn from blue jean blue to a wonderful pink color as she began breathing … and yes, screaming. Rachel Dianne Sharitz was born. A perfect miracle!

Her birth and life were true miracles from God and we both knew it. I wasn't in control at all. In fact, I was never in control. God was. I needed to work on giving up my thirst for control and start trusting God. But at the time, I didn't know how to do that. I only knew how to take control and trust my hard work, not God. Still, I'd just seen the miracle of birth and God's will. My pierced heart began wanting more from God.

We had tried so hard to have children, then just 16 months after his sister arrived, Daniel Joseph Sharitz was born at 2:30 in the morning, April 22, 1996. Daniel's healthy birth had also been a special blessing. He had been so active inside the womb, that he somehow tied an actual knot in his umbilical cord. He was born four weeks early because of this issue, but he was perfectly healthy. God kept showing us His blessings. His hands were open and waiting for me to reach out to Him.

I took a couple of weeks off to bond with Daniel. I had done the same thing with Rachel, but since Daniel was born prematurely, he had to spend a lot of time under the lights to help with jaundice issues. Thus, I didn't hold him as much as I had his sister when she was an infant. To fill up my time, I pulled out my camera and took so many photos of these amazing kiddos. *What else would a cameraman do?*

Then I got a brilliant idea. I decided to create a small brochure mailer with pictures of our beautiful baby boy to send to friends, family, clients, and most importantly, potential new clients. When I say this, I had a few potential clients in mind, but mostly I made this mailer to send to Cari.

I still wanted to win her business at the restaurant chain. I knew that during the previous two years of leaving voicemails that there were a few months where she left for maternity leave as well. She gave me this intel herself on her voicemail greeting. I figured a personal and creative card from me might trigger her motherly instincts and prompt her to finally return my call.

It worked!

Within a few days of mailing out this adorable card, I got a voicemail from Cari: "You are one persistent guy … and you truly have no shame. You're even willing to stoop so low as to play the mother card on me. Okay, we need to meet and talk about what your agency can do for our business."

I had successfully navigated this challenge. And I felt very proud of myself on controlling this victory.

12

More than I Knew

And what do you benefit if you gain the whole world but lose your own soul? Is anything worth more than your soul? (Matthew 16:26, NLT)

I ARRANGED A TIME TO MEET face-to-face with Cari, certain I could win the account. When I sat down with Cari, she said, "I can't explain why I felt I should even meet with you."

I practically cut her off, wanting to control the narrative and explain why I was so persistent. I started with a charm-filled, enthusiastic response about how we could help her franchisees and add incredible value to the brand overall. I needed her to know that we were the best, that we wouldn't be slowed down by any obstacles. As I started to jump into pitch mode, she interrupted me.

"As interested as I might be about your pitch, I need to tell you that I have this strange motherly voice telling me I need to help you be less aggressive. You want to be a value-added partner, TJ, but I need to help you be a humble value-added partner."

Ouch. Just ouch. How do you respond to this?

I was mad, hurt, and suddenly more determined to win her business. She had turned the tables on me. *What just happened?* She was now going to put effort into developing me and my character? My goal to grow her business didn't include mentoring TJ. But her clear insistence disarmed me, so I gave in. Somewhat reluctantly, I welcomed her into helping me grow.

Over the next several years, Cari patiently taught me the franchise business and how to best market different brand concepts. Beyond that, she pointed out to me every time I was arrogant and pushy. I needed her guidance more than I knew. I confessed to her how I wanted more, much more—more clients, more employees, more income, more toys.

Cari started to become concerned about my priorities and constant talk of wanting more "stuff" with never a mention of wanting more time with my wife or children. Eventually, her concerns grew into fears for me and my marriage. As much as she tried to communicate this concern to me and tried to help me see a different way for success, I was too focused on what I wanted to listen to her. If I was being honest, I felt empty. Somehow, I wanted to prove to my dead father that I was just like him. He had been a successful business owner; I needed to be one as well.

After we'd been working together for some time, the restaurant chain that Cari worked for was purchased, and she was let go from the company. Our work relationship also ended, but she was still invested in helping me grow personally. Part of her separation package included attendance at a seminar called Choices in Dallas, Texas. When she got back from the seminar, she determined that I would attend it myself. Without me knowing, she called Jaci. Jaci knew all about Cari, but they had just not had the opportunity to meet. Cari quickly got to the point, telling my wife that she was worried about me and my intense drive.

Cari told Jaci all about the Choices seminar and why she thought it was important that I attend. She was convinced it would help me get my life back in balance. She also mentioned that this seminar would be helpful for our marriage, and it would encourage my faith. Cari wasn't even sure if we were followers of Christ since I never talked about God, only myself. She was legitimately concerned for both of us—my drive for control was so bad that she saw how much wreckage could be left in my path if I didn't make some real changes.

She wasn't wrong. Jaci responded with authenticity, confessing to Cari how dissatisfied she was about how much I was working. She said that even when I was home with my family, my mind revolved around work or thinking about closing the next big deal. I had become a workaholic. I was never satisfied, constantly wanting more. There was not much joy in my heart, just an endless pursuit. And when I wasn't working or thinking about work, I turned to my hidden pastime of pornography. I had essentially stopped being a husband or a dad. To Jaci and the kids, I had turned into merely a paycheck. She figured she had nothing to lose by pushing me towards Choices' seminar. I wasn't present anyway.

With Jaci promising to encourage me to attend the seminar, Cari convinced me to go. Her clear and concise pitch to me completely spoke my language. "TJ, Choices is going to answer so many of your business questions, and it's going to help you get more of what you want." *Now that's more like it, a place where I can learn how to get more of what I want!* I agreed to go to the seminar, but only because it felt like a worthwhile investment toward my pursuit of *more.* I gladly packed my bags and jumped on a flight to Dallas to see what all this was about.

Walking into the conference room, I felt like I fit in great with this crowd. There were just over 70 people who seemed just like me, down to their business casual outfits. We all sat in a giant circle, while a dozen or so people in full suits stood outside our circle. They looked like funeral directors to me—none of them showed any emotion as they waited patiently for everyone to find their seat in the circle. Banners around the room encouraged me that we would quickly learn how to motivate sales and grow our businesses. I resonated with these signs: "Be-Do-Have" and "What I Fear, I Create." Even the Choices tagline, "Changing the world one heart at a time," hit home with me. It was time to saddle up and learn how to get more of what I want.

Eventually an older lady came out and introduced herself as the leader of the Choices seminar. She commanded the room, then quickly took the spotlight off herself by putting it on us attendees. She randomly chose different people, having them stand and share their name along with why they were attending. This went on for at least a couple of hours. It seemed to me people were open to sharing oddly vulnerable details of their messed-up lives. I started to believe I was in the wrong conference room after all. At some point, she was going to call on me and I wasn't sure what I was going to say.

My life was great. There was nothing remotely messed up for me to share. If this was the right seminar, what had Cari gotten me into?

The lady finally called on me as the last participant to share. She looked at me. “And why are you here?” I stood up and confidently said, “My name is TJ Sharitz. A client recommended I attend a wonderful business seminar to help me discover more tools for me to grow my advertising agency into its full potential. I am afraid that I ended up in the wrong room, however. I didn’t want to be rude and walk out while you all were bravely sharing about your lives, but I don’t have any issues because my life is great. So, if you’ll excuse me, I will head off to find where I am supposed to be.”

Apparently, this speech gave her a lot of information about me. With a big grin, she asked, “Since you have no issues, what’s the biggest decision you are facing right now?” I told her I was trying to figure out how much bigger an office space to rent.

“What’s the worst thing that can happen if you make the wrong decision?”

“I could end up going into debt, which would challenge my ability to be profitable.”

“What’s the worst thing that could happen if you went into debt and lost profits?”

“Well, I could become bankrupt.”

I started to see where this was going.

“What’s the worst thing that could happen if you became bankrupt?”

“I’m pretty certain my wife and kids would leave me because I would be a failure and a loser.”

"Well, what's the worst thing that could happen if they left you?"

The tone of my voice instantly changed as I became agitated, "I would probably become homeless. I would get some kind of disease, not be able to get any medical care, and die all alone. I would be … all alone."

She thanked me for sharing and assured me I was in the right seminar. I felt kind of broken at that moment. I had no idea all that was lying below the surface, pushing me to have control of every single aspect of my life.

I sat there contemplating how this fear of failure had taken over my whole life. Ever since that day playing football in my yard and finding out I had dyslexia, I was convinced I would be a failure in life unless I could manufacture wins. Not just a few victories, but a win at every single opportunity. I had been living as if one little loss would make the whole thing crumble beneath me. I couldn't trust anyone, especially God, to protect or take care of me. I had to build everything for myself and there was no amount of stuff in the world that was going to satisfy me.

While at the Choices seminar, I was given the nick name of "Almost a Man," as a result from my sharing with the group. I accepted it as a fitting, albeit insulting, nickname. Ends up I had been living my life trying to prove myself to my dad who had died 11 years earlier. I had built my own successful small business like him, owned a Mercedes Benz like him, became a dad like him. I even one upped him, owning a gold Submariner Rolex watch. I soon discovered I could never fill that void and become a "man." That void could only be filled with Jesus. I desperately needed Him to fill it so I could live free with grace, peace, and love.

Our homework that night was to write down a 65-item gripe list, followed by a 65-item gratitude list, on our own with no help. I wasn't pumped about the thought of homework, but my roommate and I sat in our room trying our best to get the assignment done. My roommate shared with me how he had attempted to take his own life two times before coming to this seminar. I supposed with that reality, he had no problems coming up with a full list of gripes. However, he struggled intensely to come up with even five things he was grateful for. I was just the opposite. I spent most of the night writing down blessings and things I was truly grateful for. My list went far beyond 65. The more I wrote, the more it felt like the hardened shell around my heart was being chiseled away … and I had no control over it. It felt amazing.

As I continued to pour my heart onto the pages, it occurred to me that I needed to call Jaci to share what I was learning. My call went straight to voicemail, so I left her a heartfelt message about my new self-discoveries. I asked her to please forgive me, then broke down crying with tears of remorse and joy. I shared about my many blessings and her unwavering love for me. I promised her that I was going to spend the next several days getting my life back on track, with promises of reconnecting with God. I had also discovered I had to make some big changes in my life right away. I needed God in my life, and I had to spend quality time with her and the kids. I hung up, then called Cari, leaving her a similar message thanking her for tricking me into going to this "business" seminar, for helping me to get my life back in the right order.

The Choices seminar finished up four days later, with many hearts being changed for the good, including mine. I took a new "heartfelt" control. Instead of flying back home to Atlanta, right back to the same old routines and bad habits, I changed my ticket to fly up north to surprise Jaci and the kids on their vacation at Moon Lake in Wisconsin.

I originally chartered a seaplane to fly me directly to the lake from the airport, anticipating a spectacular splash entrance. But black skies and a nearby tornado ruined that plan. Instead, I rented a car and drove through a downpour to the tiny town of Turtle Lake, Wisconsin, near Moon Lake. Since I didn't have the cabin's actual address, my hope and prayer were to drive around the lake and hopefully find her car at her parents' cabin.

I drove over to the lake and turned down a small gravel road that dead ended into a road with cabins on it. I took a wild guess, turned left, and within a couple of cabins found Jaci's Jeep parked in the driveway. I did a fist bump in the air. "Thank you, Jesus, for guiding me right to their cabin."

To say the very least, my surprise appearance resulted in great joy and celebration by all. Both Jaci and her parents were thankful that my experience at the seminar had empowered me to change my priorities, placing God first, spending more time with my family and being present in the moment. We spent the next week playing on the lake, attending the local fair, and making s'mores over the campfires each night. I thought my heart was changed forever.

13

Disappointed and Doubtful

Therefore, if anyone is in Christ, he is a new creation; the old has gone; the new has come! (2 Corinthians 5:17, NIV)

I FELT CLOSE TO GOD WHEN I was a little boy. I knew He was *with* me and was *for* me. When the dyslexia bomb dropped in third grade, I could not understand it. I already felt such shame about the secret I was hiding, of what someone else had done to me, that I will discuss in due time in this book. If God was for me, how could He have let this happen to me? Over time, I had become very angry at Him, blaming Him and my parents for all my struggles and pain. I couldn't reconcile why God would allow bad stuff to happen to me if He was as good as everyone said He was.

God seemed untrustworthy to me—I couldn't trust Him to provide, guide, or protect me. I *clearly* had to look out for myself. If I didn't assume control of things, who knows what bad stuff I would have encountered. This created a work ethic and a drive that reinforced the notion that I had to be in control of everything. Every. Single. Thing.

It was an imperative to be in total control of my life. It felt logical. If I'm not in control, who else would be?

Others had wanted to label me as "retarded" or "challenged." With that label, I would have been run over by inconsiderate and uncaring teachers or bosses every single day. There would have been an endless list of *things I couldn't do* because I lacked the ability or capacity. Just ask the Kiwanis keynote speaker.

I often wonder how my life would have turned out if I hadn't pursued total control of everything. Would I have graduated from high school, gone to college, or become an athlete (who was one Charlie Brown kick away from being a professional)? I doubt I could have married such a great woman, probably wouldn't have opened a business. I can't prove any of this, but it seemed obvious to me that I willed all this stuff into existence, not God.

If you had asked me before the Choices seminar about my belief in God, I would have answered "I believe in Him." While this was moderately true, it wasn't something I lived my life by. The truth of the matter was I had no gratitude for God because I didn't need Him.

I have a theory that we are most grateful for the things in our life that we believe we need. Jaci is a great example of this. I am very thankful for her—I wish I could have said that prior to the Choices seminar I attended. For many years, I didn't realize how much I needed her, but I'm so thankful I realize this now. Before then, however, our marriage was not good because of my lack of awareness. I shudder to think what might have happened with us if I hadn't listened to Cari and gone to the seminar. It did change things for me and our marriage. Not perfect, but better.

I also can admit that prior to Choices, I had stayed angry at God.

I blamed Him for all my struggles and pain. I was a victim. He felt far away and uncaring. I did not trust that God had my best interest in mind or if He had any idea what would be in my best interest, for that matter. At the time, the only explanation I had was that God hated me, or He was angry right back at me for whatever reason. I was God's exception; God had made junk when He created me.

I know now that this is not true, but that was how I secretly felt for a good portion of my life. Doing the gratitude list at the seminar caused me to take a moment, slow down and think; it changed my perspective in significant ways. I was challenged to recognize how much I needed my Lord and Savior. Most of those things on my gratitude list? I didn't deserve them. I certainly hadn't earned them. The opposite, in fact. It was kind of a miracle I had so many things to be grateful for. I wasn't doing as fine on my own as I thought, and I needed a lot of help.

That night in my room when I was writing this gratitude list, I found myself drawn to a particular set of scripture in 2 Corinthians 5:16-21. Here is the gist of it. When we let go of control and live life as if we belong to Christ, the old life is over and the new life officially begins. This is a gift from God. Jesus is a gift from God. He is the perfect sacrifice for our sins because He never sinned. I know this might be odd or confusing, but we are reconciled to God because of this gift. When we live in this "new life" we can help other people be reconciled as well.

I had been living fully in my "old life," trying to fill my need for reconciliation with performance and success. It was not working for me. It was never going to work. As the famous saying goes, "We all have a God-shaped hole in our hearts." I tried filling it with anything other than God. That realization broke me that night as I read those verses in 2 Corinthians. I discovered that even though I had blamed God and turned away from Him, He did not hold my sins against me. I experienced God in an exhilarating, new way that night. I couldn't wait to start my new life.

There's another famous quote that says we are to "preach the Gospel at all times … use words if necessary." It's laughable to me how far I was from all of that. The old TJ method was to "stay in control at all times … seek God only when necessary." I literally used God as if I just needed to break the glass in an emergency.

I am guessing you are reading a book about control because you struggle with the same thing or know someone who does. I'm certain just about every human being on earth has struggled with control at one time or another. I suppose it comforts me a little to know I am in good company, knowing that wanting to wield control is a problem.

In Louie Giglio's book *Winning the War on Worry*, he nails us fellow control freaks, "Our shoulders were never meant for total control." He goes on to point out that "control is actually quicksand, pulling us further under, where we begin to worry," concluding we should operate in love, for "His love leads to surrender, and surrender leads to trust."[2]

God knew I needed to surrender, that I would need Him more than ever when death came for me. At the time, I had no idea how much I was going to need to trust in Him.

After I returned home from the Choices seminar, I began regularly relenting, repenting, receiving, and rejoicing (even a dyslexic can enjoy good alliteration). For the next four months or so, I flew back to Texas every month to volunteer at Choices as a facilitator. I wanted Jaci to experience the same seminar so she could understand my experience better. Plus, I desired for her to have that growth as well. She agreed to go, but she didn't have much hope our lives would change in any significant way.

After so many years of me putting all my energy into work and needing to control everything, Jaci had grown weary of being disappointed. She agreed to go to the seminar because she had seen *some* change in me and she wanted to support that, but she was doubtful she would gain anything from the workshop.

Thankfully, we both learned several important lessons that week. Jaci realized she had formed opinions about me without a full understanding of how my brain works. She had been coping with my control, while at the same time building resentment for me. In her mind, she thought I didn't care enough about her to listen to her or to care about what she said.

One of the facilitators had us do an exercise where we sat on the floor, facing each other and holding hands. She asked Jaci to tell me three things that she did that morning, and I was to repeat them back to her. She chose three simple things like, "I took a shower, then I ate eggs and an English muffin, and then I practiced my song with my group." I quickly began to repeat them back to her—and I couldn't. I wasn't distracted or not trying. I honestly tried. The entire group watched us as I struggled to recall the three basic things my wife had just told me. All these years Jaci thought I just didn't care to remember what she asked of me or shared with me. Now, as we did this exercise, her eyes opened. She understood that I honestly couldn't remember what she had told me. That day my wife got a clearer glimpse of how my dyslexia impacts me.

At that seminar, Jaci also realized she had been making judgments about me unfairly. Her father was the spiritual head of their family, and he had a strong faith. He gave intentionally to the church, gave his time volunteering in Camp Fire Girls, coached the neighborhood swim team as a volunteer. Most of all, he loved Jaci's mother as Christ loved the Church. He was the textbook definition of a servant husband and father. Jaci thought all Christian husbands were like her dad, and I was failing her miserably. My good friend and fellow author Jim Barnard calls this an "expectation gap" in his book, *The Suffering Guy*.[3] With my high expectations for building a successful business on one side and Jaci's expectations of me being a godly husband and father on the other, our expectation gap had been getting larger by the day and we had no idea.

Jaci also learned that she had contributed to my disappointing her as a husband and father by not sharing the things that were hurting her in our relationship and family life.

It was a wakeup call for both of us. I had no idea how much I had been disappointing my wife. I didn't blame her. I'd been so blind to her needs, it's no wonder she felt the way she did. Jaci had kept a lot of this from me. They say, "You only know what you know" and "You see what you want to see." I knew nothing, and from my perspective, I saw a great marriage. When Jaci shared her disappointment with me, I was blown away, brought to tears, humbled, and grateful for her being my best friend and wife. I had no idea how poorly I was treating her and the kids, or that our marriage was on thin ice before I went to Choices the first time. Jaci's heartfelt words opened my eyes and my heart. We left Texas together, excited about making more improvements in our marriage and family life.

While all that sounds great and promising for a future of preaching the Gospel with and without words, reality showed up and slapped us hard, challenging both of us and our marriage. I'm not proud to admit that this newfound dependence on God after the seminar was short lived. Extremely short lived.

14

It's About Time

Humble yourselves, therefore, under God's mighty hand, that he may lift you up in due time. (1 Peter 5:6, NIV)

WE STARTED ATTENDING CHURCH AGAIN. Jaci and I worked more as a parental team with Rachel and Daniel. I continued to work hard in my business, but I made a play space for the children in the back of my office to allow more time together. Our future looked more promising.

I'd learned how much I needed God in my life, but at the same time I continued to pursue status and collect the "toys" that reflected my financial success. It was as if I constantly had to prove I could be a winner in life with a great business, beautiful home, beautiful family, wonderful vacations, and great cars.

I had built a successful business, but I controlled every aspect of the business, more like a micromanager and less like a leader. Of course, I tried to control everything in our home as well. Even though my eyes had been opened at the seminar, the thought of losing control over a situation remained stressful for me—like you can't breathe, like life or death. It was that strong.

Although Jaci and I made progress after she attended the workshop, when it came down to Jaci's way or my way, she continued to defer to my wishes. So, when I wanted to continue to leave her and the kids once each month to fly to Texas or Vancouver and serve as a facilitator at seminars at our own expense, she agreed. What else could she do? I framed it as giving back, and it was that, but I must admit I had a lot of fun on these trips while Jaci was home alone taking care of the house, kids, and two large dogs.

It was on a morning after getting home from a seminar in June 2000 that I woke up with intense back pain, the explosion that felt like a knife stab or a gunshot wound. When I was asked at my first Choices seminar the question "What's the worst thing that can happen?" and I answered that I could get sick and die, I had no idea how close that would be to coming true. And more than once.

The urgent care doctor said the tests didn't show anything wrong with me, but after several days of pain meds, bedrest, and relentless pain, I knew something wasn't right. I had no medical history of any health issues, but when the intense back pain persisted, it no longer made sense this was a simple back strain from facilitating at a recent seminar.

I called to make another appointment, this time with my longtime primary care doctor. He was a good friend and one of Jaci's co-workers, so I knew I could trust him. After examining me carefully, he suspected I had a herniated disc. He recommended physical therapy along with a stronger anti-inflammatory and a new pain med.

I eagerly started physical therapy the very next day, hopeful they would be able to fix me and relieve the intolerable pain. Despite the stronger medications, when my newly assigned physical therapist worked with me on my first visit, I literally cried out in pain every time he tried to bend or move me. My yelling due to discomfort got so bad, they ended up reassigning me to a back room away from the other patients so I wouldn't scare or upset them.

The morning after my first attempt at physical therapy, I woke up so sore and stiff I could barely get out of bed. Jaci had to help me get to the bathroom and then back into the bedroom so I could lie on the floor to do my home physical therapy exercises. I lay on the floor with sheer determination to compose myself, to not focus on the pain. I was becoming more disabled by the hour from this relentless back pain with no relief in sight.

My home PT exercises were simple and straight forward—lay face down and push my chest off the floor to help my spine re-align and relieve the pressure on my herniated disc. Our two small children, Rachel and Daniel, rushed in and lay down to join me during "workout time." They'd do ten pushups while I struggled to push my chest off the floor in one stretching manner. They seemed so proud of themselves for how much stronger they were than me. I tried my best not to be annoyed when they jumped up and flexed in my face to show off their muscles. It was actually pretty cute, but it was hard to acknowledge their cuteness at that exact excruciating moment.

A few days later, they joined me again on the floor of my bedroom, but this time I couldn't move my chest off the floor at all. As hard as I tried, I couldn't get a single inch off the floor. It scared me to death. Rachel saw the fear on my face. She ran to Jaci in the other room. I heard her scream, "Daddy's dying!"

There was no way I was going to let her believe that, so I mustered up all the strength I could to put on a happy face. When they both ran into the room, I assured them I felt a lot better. I said I was just worn out from all the effort I was putting into the therapy. I really wanted to believe I was getting better, but I wasn't, and it petrified me.

I went to see a chiropractor the following week. I felt good about trusting him with my back issues since it was his expertise. The doctor confirmed, based on the x-rays he had taken of my back, that nothing was structurally wrong with my spine. His conclusion was that the pain and lack of mobility had to be muscular. He assured me it would get better with time. I took that information to Jaci and convinced her (and myself) that I was improving. I didn't want her to cancel her upcoming vacation with the kids to visit their grandparents at the lake in Wisconsin.

In reality, I continued to get weaker and less mobile by the day. I had no idea what was going on with my back. I struggled to believe I had a muscular problem, since the pain medication was doing absolutely nothing to dull the intense pain. I wasn't sleeping at all during the night. I felt so out of control. I kept telling myself I needed to *Man up, cupcake.* My pep talks failed to give me any actual encouragement.

Jaci arranged for one of our close neighbor friends to stop by our house to check on me while she was away with the kids. I kept insisting this wasn't necessary, but she wasn't buying it. In the afternoons, he would help me walk slowly down the street to our neighborhood pool where I'd just float on a noodle for an hour or so. Floating in the pool seemed to be the only thing that ever gave me any relief from the pain. After a couple days, our friend noticed that I seemed to be visibly losing weight. He insisted on helping me get on the scale, which revealed I had lost more than 30 pounds over the previous few weeks. This was not good. When Jaci heard about this, she cut short her vacation and rushed back home to Georgia.

As soon as Jaci saw me, she knew I was seriously ill and called my doctor. He ordered an emergency MRI to see if there was something more they were missing. The MRI showed osteomyelitis (a bone infection) in my spine, so the doctor ordered an immediate bone biopsy. This wasn't fun at all. It involved making a small cut in my skin over the infected vertebrae, then placing a needle into the bone to cut out and remove a small sample of it. Results confirmed I had a severe bacterial infection in my spinal column, as well as an abscess that had spread across my lower back.

My doctor explained the urgency. He was transferring my case to an infectious disease specialist. While shaking his head, the doctor told Jaci they would do everything possible to save me. *What? That escalated quickly!*

I wanted to scream to the doctor, "You have got to be kidding me. I can't die. I am too young. I can't leave my wife and kids. I have followed every direction from every doctor, and this is where it ends? Please, just give me some relief from the pain and I can finally get some sleep. I will be fine if I can just get some sleep!"

The next day we drove to meet the infectious disease specialist to learn more about this infection, to hopefully get a less dramatic take on its severity. After reviewing all the test results and imaging, he told us he would treat me aggressively with different antibiotics. And since this was terminal—*Did he just say "terminal"?* —he would prescribe three much stronger pain medications, the weakest being Fentanyl. He followed with a clear directive that I needed to get my affairs in order right away. *What do you mean, "get my affairs in order?" This is that serious?* He shifted his tone to communicate compassion in this next statement, "The question isn't *if* this bacterial bone infection is going to kill you, but how quickly it will do so. No one has ever survived this bacterial infection before. It is that fatal."

How do you respond to *that?* I didn't believe him, didn't want to believe him. But this was the second doctor to say something like this. *It's got to be real. How did I get here?* I wondered if the outcome would be different if this problem had been spotted earlier. What did I do to deserve this? I went to several doctors and followed their direction precisely. Now I am going to die? Is God in control here? What about all the changes I'd been making? I was volunteering for seminars at my own expense, spending more time with the family, even trying to trust Him more. Was it too little too late? Or does He still hate me that much? Will He even let me into heaven? All of this was impossible to process fully. One thing I did know—being told to get "my affairs in order" created a need to wield control again.

Jaci was a pharmacist. She dealt with stuff like this all the time, and even she looked clueless on how to respond. The infectious disease doctor attempted to give us a game plan through this mess. He said he was going to do everything he could to try to stop the progression of the infection within the next three weeks. *If I lived that long*, he added. At that point, he would order another MRI to see if the progression of the infection had been halted or not. Because my immune system was so weakened by this infection, he wanted me to remain at home and not go to the hospital unless it was unavoidable, since I could be potentially exposed to something else there.

At home, Jaci was an excellent nurse for me. She administered IV antibiotics into my bloodstream around the clock, plus all kinds of powerful pain medications designed to give some amount of comfort to those in the most desperate levels of pain. She fed me, changed my clothes, helped me to the bathroom, and never dropped a single ball as a mother. This was not what she signed up for. Rachel and Daniel were five and four respectively. They needed both their parents but could only have their mom when she was not knee deep in caring for me. I could tell Jaci was maxed out. How could she not be scared and overwhelmed, with little hope of me surviving? She seemed superhuman to me at that point. How she didn't fall apart during all of it is beyond my understanding. I doubt I could have handled it a quarter as well as she did if she had been the one with the mysterious infection.

My wife would tell you she was a broken-down mess. I don't see it that way, but I can understand why she felt that way—it was an unbelievable burden for her to carry. She finally stepped outside of her comfort zone, reaching out for help from the ladies in our neighborhood. We didn't know them all that well since we were newer to the neighborhood, but they showed up in force. They organized meal delivery to our home every other day and checked in with Jaci constantly. These ladies made a gigantic difference when my family needed them the most.

As we approached the end of the three weeks, I was still alive, but barely. Despite the specialist's aggressive treatment, the pain in my back had become worse and I had lost all mobility in my legs. I couldn't have imagined it could get any worse; it already was more than I could handle. The Fentanyl patch, approved for treating advanced cancer or terminal illness like mine, is over 50 times more potent than morphine, yet it did little to relieve my pain. The doctor had also added Meperidine, another opioid because it works in the brain to change how your body feels and responds to pain. Not my brain. Finally, he prescribed Flexeril (cyclobenzaprine), a muscle relaxant that works by blocking nerve impulses (or pain sensations) that are sent to your brain. Fentanyl and Meperidine are highly addictive and should not be used long-term, but the doctor knew my pain required something this strong before I died. Even with the powerful, addictive pain meds my doctor had prescribed to help get some relief, the pain remained unbearable. I felt desperate with no hope in sight.

The illness in my life caused me to walk back everything I had committed myself to. Suddenly there was no gratitude or healthy spiritual perspective. My overly busy mind kept me in a vicious cycle of fear and anxiety. I feared falling asleep because I wasn't sure if I would die in my sleep or wake up alone in intense pain, unable to do anything about it. I was frustrated beyond all hope.

I began to think dark thoughts about ending things before it could get any further out of hand. But I had no ability to move on my own, other than my hands. What was I going to do, hold my breath?

After three weeks on these meds, Jaci had to take me for a follow-up MRI. While I waited for her to take the kids to stay with a neighbor while we were at the hospital, I lay in bed all alone, exhausted and in total misery. In desperation, I looked up to God and yelled at Him. "God, send me to hell, or take me to heaven right now! Dragging this out is not fair to Jaci or the kids."

I've heard of other people praying prayers like: "If You save me ... I'll go back to church. I'll stop sleeping around. I won't drink again. I will be devoted to You forever." I believe this is called bargaining. Bargaining is just a last-ditch effort to retain control, a prayer that promises devotion if God delivers in a time of extreme need. It's a realization that all your efforts and determination have gotten you to a point where no amount of effort or determination will resolve anything. You are trapped and there is no way out on your own. That is exactly what I was doing with God, trying to bargain my way to a conclusion on this death sentence. I didn't care which way God chose; I just needed it to be done and over with. *Now!* Things were that bad.

I am not sure why it took me so long to get to this point, but I finally got real with God. I had to admit I had no control of anything. At the same time, it seemed like God didn't either, or if He did, He was clearly enjoying messing with me.

With what little strength I had left, I screamed at God. "This is between You and me, God. You must hate me because I want to control everything. I haven't trusted You and I can't trust You right now."

I laid it all on the table. No holding back. I was completely helpless and hopeless. I needed to be rescued.

"I can't keep doing this. I give up. I am good as dead and there's not a single thing I can do about it. So do what You need to do … what You *want* to do. Please do it now before Jaci gets back. Send me to hell or bring me to sit with You. I am dead. The only way I can live is if You live in me. I totally surrender to You, once and for all—I will surrender. The choice is Yours. But I give up."

This is where I found myself. The only act of control left for me to wield was to choose to yield it. I am not great with words, but this clever wordplay connects with me: *wield* control or *yield* control. Not just because I was in that moment praying a prayer of desperation, but because this had been a lifelong journey of wrestling with control. That day I relinquished control at last, placing myself squarely in God's control, with no clue what would happen next. It was my own "Come to Jesus" moment.

When Jaci got back from the neighbor's house, she took one quick look at me on the bed and cried out, "Oh my God, what have you done? I wasn't gone that long! Oh my God."

I wasn't sure how to answer her question, not confident I could muster up the strength to respond in any way. I thought I possibly was in hell because this couldn't be heaven. I felt convinced I was going to be stuck on my back for all of eternity, listening to Jaci ask me the same questions, over and over again. (For the record, listening to Jaci talk is the furthest thing from hell I could ever conceive of. I was just so messed up in the head and scared that nothing made sense.)

Jaci ran over to our dresser, grabbed a mirror, and shoved it in front of me, yelling, "Look at your face! Your color is back, and you even have the twinkle back in your eyes."

My vision was a little fuzzy right then, so I couldn't quite see what she was seeing.

"What did you do in the few minutes I was gone?"

How do I explain this to her? Would she believe me? Do I even believe this?

"I surrendered to God."

I braced for impact, thinking she would be mad or confused. Instead, she came over and gave me a gigantic hug.

She started to cry. "It's about time! Why do you always need to control everything? You never let anyone help you, especially God. Why couldn't you just let go faster?"

I am a blessed man to have such a wonderful, loving, and strong Christian wife.

Later, when we got the results from that day's MRI and met with my infectious disease doctor, he exclaimed, "It's a miracle, TJ! I think we can save your life." He explained that the infection hadn't only slowed down—it had completely stopped in its tracks.

I know there are other people who have had circumstances just as hard, or harder, who have bargained with God in a similar way. Whether or not others have received this kind of miracle in return, I don't know, but a miracle did happen for me. A part of me felt guilty for having this privilege when others have experienced different outcomes. I cannot understand or explain it, but I know it happened.

While it would be possible to dissect the validity of how this mysterious infection stopped spreading, I think it is more beneficial to ponder over the response Jaci gave me when I fessed up to what I did while she was gone. It is fascinating that she believed me when I said that I surrendered to God.

I think most people would say, "Come again? What did you do?" They would probably assume they misheard my answer because it makes no sense. It makes no sense to me; why would it make any sense to anyone else? I could also understand a statement of disbelief. "Okay sure, you *surrendered* to God and now you are *healed*, and I am the Stay Puff Marshmallow Man." I could handle that kind of sarcasm. Knowing Jaci, I would have expected her to ask me to clarify my answer, like, "What does that mean exactly?" Questions to give her context to what I had experienced. But she didn't. Instead …

"It's about time!"

I knew exactly what she was talking about. For most of my life, fear had driven my desperate need to always be in control. Yes, I had made huge strides in my relationship with God, especially through Choices, and she was there for all of that. In fact, my growing intimacy with God was the answer to her prayers. But I had still held onto a deep-rooted need for control. Now I had finally let go and let God take control. I'm grateful He let me live.

15

Big Deal or Not

I shall not die, but I shall live, and recount the deeds of the Lord. (Psalm 118:17, ESV)

After God spared my life, it might sound like I figured it all out when it came to yielding control to God. Oh, how I wish that was true. I did improve quite a bit, but my humanity still got in the way. It still does sometimes, to be completely honest. I can say that when I successfully trusted God to be in total control of everything, it gave me a real sense of freedom. I began to find it challenging to deny the Lord what was His—me. I belonged to him. He was in control of everything—including my life. *Amen! Thank you, God, for your faithfulness, even when I was faithless.* I'd finally, after 40 years, truly surrendered all control to God and He showed me mercy, grace, and unconditional love. I could no longer deny Him. God was in total control, and I loved that freedom.

Despite the miracle that had just happened, I still had plenty of medical challenges to navigate. The toll this infection took on my body still needed to be addressed, especially as I had no immune system to speak of at the time. During the next phase of treatment, a home health nurse came to the house twice a week to administer different drugs. Jaci legitimately could have administered the drugs to me herself, but she deserved a break.

One particular visit from the nurse did not go the way I would have expected. Her visits were normally short and unexciting. This time she noticed the beginning signs of yeast at my dual PICC line entrance into my arm. At first, she tried to talk herself out of the possibility of it, choosing to stay focused on pushing the medication through. But she kept coming back to inspect the PICC site. I could tell something was not right.

"What's up?"

"Um, I hate to say this, but I think you guys should go to the emergency room right away." She suspected that a yeast infection had developed in the PICC line and feared it could get into my blood stream. That would most likely kill me since I was already so immune compromised.

Jaci and the nurse helped me into the car to head to the ER. As Jaci backed out of the garage, I talked myself into my own understanding: *This is not a big deal.* All they had to do was move the PICC line into my other arm. Normally, I would have freaked out and tried to do something to wield control. I don't know what that would have been in this circumstance, but I don't underestimate my ability to figure something out.

A few moments into our drive toward the hospital, I felt God tell me everything was going to be okay. It's always a big deal when you sense or hear from God. I should have grabbed Jaci's hand and told her about the message from God, but I just sat there like a meathead. I think I was doubting I'd truly heard from God. A good friend of mine often says that he gets confused between God and gas: Both give him "tummy troubles." I think he's referring mostly to the things God reveals that go against our human plans and desires. In this instance, I wasn't getting any tummy troubles; I was receiving peace throughout my body. It had to be God reassuring me. I sensed this was important to share with Jaci, but I didn't.

A couple minutes later the skies opened, and it began to pour down rain so hard we could barely see. The windshield wipers worked as fast as they could, pushing away gallons of water every second. Jaci did her best to stay calm, a challenge given the circumstances and the intensity of the rain. Neither of us had ever seen anything like it. Suddenly, we heard a loud noise. Our car jerked to the right and the steering wheel began to vibrate vigorously. We had blown a tire at high speed in the rain. Jaci handled it like a champ. She instinctively put her blinker on and moved over to the emergency lane, despite all the traffic speeding by us.

As we came to a stop, I then jokingly said to God, "Lord, I know we need the rain, but if you would make this rain stop for us it would make things so much easier for Jaci changing the tire." When I opened the door, the rain immediately stopped. I got chills up and down my spine as I let go of the door handle. In fact, I've got them right now as I share this story with you. This was so unbelievable to me that I started wondering if the pain drugs were causing me to hallucinate. No way. God stopped the rain for us.

Unfortunately, this infection nonsense caused me to lose the ability to use my legs. My muscles atrophied, stiffening my legs to the point where I could not move around by myself. They were also numb. During this time, I had to use a walker to hold myself up. Since I could not move my legs, Daniel would hang out under the bar of the walker and move my feet for me. It was extremely painful and embarrassing. I was a grown man who couldn't get around by himself because the infection over time had blocked my nerves to my lower body and legs. So, in this circumstance of needing to help Jaci change the tire, my only plan was to lean against the side of the car and bark out instructions.

Jaci came around to my side, helped me out of the car with my IV bags, and helped me get to the trunk so I could talk her through changing the tire. There was a reasonable chance my plea to God and the rain stopping as God's response was all real, and I should take a moment to tell Jaci that God answered my prayer request. It felt too significant not to celebrate, but once again I didn't because I wasn't sure if she would believe it. Plus, she seemed a little overwhelmed.

As she was getting the spare out, I decided to test God again. "God, if you really did stop the rain, it would be great if you would have a trooper stop and change the tire for us. Do this and I promise, as soon as I'm well, I'll take our family back to church." Yes, I was bargaining with God again.

"Look T, there's a trooper pulling over to help us."

The officer got out of his car and exclaimed, "Did y'all see that rain just stop? That was a real gulley washer in the middle of this drought. It was like someone just asked God to stop the rain and it stopped immediately. Wow, what a day!" After he said that, he got straight to work on changing our tire for us like it was no big deal.

This freaked me out to no end. I wasn't dreaming or hallucinating any of this. I should have thrown a party right there on the side of the road because of what had just happened. Jaci gave me a look that told me she found it odd as well. At this point, I knew I should speak up and tell this trooper my story of three instances where God answered my prayer, and how he was specifically an answer to prayer by showing up at the exact right moment. He had teed it up for me by acknowledging the possibility that God's hand was involved. But I remained silent.

It didn't matter if the trooper believed in God or not. If he did, knowing all that God had just done for us would be incredibly edifying for him. If he didn't have faith in God and was simply saying that sarcastically, this would have been an amazing opportunity to share about God's personal way of working in our lives. This moment could not have been clearer to me, even if all the electronic signs on the highway had started flashing, "TJ, don't deny me!" That is what I was doing by not acknowledging or celebrating how the Holy Spirit was working.

I denied God three times. Looking back on this now, it totally destroys my heart. After all I had endured, having a true moment of surrender, God saving my life, and now experiencing Him specifically answering my prayers … what do I do? Rejoice and sing His praise? No, I did the exact opposite. I was apathetic and indifferent.

I "Petered out" by not having the courage to speak up. Just like the disciple Peter, I denied God three times.

Here's Peter's story in the Bible:

> And as Peter was below in the courtyard, one of the servant girls of the high priest came, and seeing Peter warming himself, she looked at him and said, 'You also were with the Nazarene, Jesus.' But he denied it, saying, 'I neither know nor understand what you mean.' And he went out into the gateway and the rooster crowed. And the servant girl saw him and began again to say to the bystanders, 'This man is one of them.' But again, he denied it. And after a little while the bystanders again said to Peter, 'Certainly you are one of them, for you are a Galilean.' But he began to invoke a curse on himself and to swear, 'I do not know this man of whom you speak.' And immediately the rooster crowed a second time. And Peter remembered how Jesus had said to him, 'Before the rooster crows twice, you will deny me three times.' And he broke down and wept. (Mark 14: 66-72, ESV)

Peter was one of the closest disciples to Jesus. The Messiah had shown him incredible favor by letting him experience unimaginable things. Jesus helped Peter walk on water, even if it was just for a few seconds. Jesus invited him to be a spectator at the transfiguration when Christ had a conversation with the Father, Moses, and Elijah. Jesus even repaired the ear that Peter cut off the side of a soldier's head in a moment of Peter's extreme zealousness. These experiences were absurd, but they were real, and Peter witnessed them all firsthand.

I feel such a kinship with Peter. He was a fellow knucklehead who chose to wield control. At the most important time, when Jesus was standing trial that would lead to His crucifixion, Peter denied his relationship with the Son of God. Jesus even told him that he would do this ahead of time, and yet Peter still did it, even though he insisted he would never *ever* do such a thing. Peter is my homeboy. We get each other. He gives me hope that Jesus won't give up on me despite my clear and obvious issues.

Peter went on to do amazing things to help build the church. He was truly the rock in ushering in a new era of living with the guidance of the Holy Spirit who chooses to dwell inside of us when we yield control to Him.

If it's real that God chose to use Peter (and I'm convinced it's real), then there is hope that God would choose to use a knucklehead like me.

16

The Whole Time

Jesus said to him, "Get up, take up your bed, and walk."
(John 5:8, ESV)

I HAD PLACED A SPECIAL ORDER for a set of new ZR rated high-performance 21-inch Michelin Sport tires for my AMG Mercedes Benz car before my illness hit. They had arrived, but when I got sick, I totally forgot them. As a result, the tires on my car were in terrible shape when we got the flat on the way to the ER.

When we finally arrived at the ER, Jaci dropped me off and drove over to the tire shop. They mounted, balanced, and checked the alignment on all four new tires. Unfortunately for me, I had only ordered the tires and not paid for them. So, Jaci gave them her credit card to cover the balance. Let's just say when she saw the final bill, she almost hit the floor. She also found out how much I had paid for my custom 21-inch rims.

I had been using my business accounts to keep Jaci in the dark about my car's "special" add-ons and other toy purchases. Now I was busted.

The ER doors swung open. "Where is he?" Jaci growled. In an instant, doctors and nurses around me disappeared, leaving me alone to face her. She confronted me with the receipt for the tires. She was very upset, but mostly disappointed with me for hiding things from her. I had not been honest or transparent with her because I knew she wouldn't have agreed to much of my foolish spending. I just really loved having a nice car with super cool rims. She let it go in that moment, as we obviously had bigger issues to deal with related to my illness. Good thing I was in the ER.

A few months after getting the PICC line yeast infection dealt with, I went to see an orthopedic surgeon to schedule two surgeries. The first one was to drain the abscess in my lower back where the nerves come together before entering the spine, then regraft some nerves for my legs. The goal of this surgery was to help me possibly regain use of my legs, which I was a gigantic fan of. The second surgery was to remove two damaged discs in my spine and fuse the three vertebrae together.

Not being able to get around by myself was the absolute worst part of the entire ordeal. My kids needed me in so many ways. I hadn't been around much when they were younger because I'd been chasing down success at work. And now, they had me at home, but I couldn't get down on the floor with them to play. It felt so unfair.

I still had a lot of back pain because of everything, but if I had to choose only one of the surgeries, I would choose the one that gave me the potential of walking again. To be clear, there was no speculation that I would be able to walk independently. I'd been informed I would most likely have to use braces on my legs. I didn't care what it took, my lack of ability to get around on my own was too much for me to handle.

The day before meeting with the surgeon, I went to the hospital to get another full-body MRI that would show my current back situation. Throughout my illness I had numerous MRIs, always with my eyes closed tightly. The morning, getting what I thought was my last MRI *ever* to show the surgeon the current condition of my back, I asked the tech to please let me know just before he started to roll me out. I wanted to see if I really was claustrophobic or not. When the tech told me he was done and ready to roll me out, I opened my eyes. *Oh my God!* I started to panic right away. I began to sweat and yelled, “Get me out of here fast!” The MRI tube almost touched my face, my chest, and arms. I was freaking out in this tiny space. The joke was totally on me; I ended up having not one, but two MRIs the next day.

When I went to the office the next day to meet with the surgeon, I gave him a copy of my MRI from the previous day. To my dismay, a technician took me for another MRI because the surgeon preferred to use his own imaging for guiding his operations. After the MRI was done, I waited for someone to help me off the table and back into my wheelchair, but no one came.

The technician finally came in and told me I would need to do it all over again. There was something wrong with these new images. I wasn’t insanely upset about this, but I also wasn’t happy about it. Staying still for an MRI was miserable for me. I worked extra hard to stay completely still, eyes closed of course, so I wouldn’t run the risk of having to do this another time.

When I got back into the office where Jaci had been waiting for me, the doctor quickly walked in and put my original MRI image up on the wall light box. He pointed out the widespread spine infection and large abscess mass in my lower back. Then he placed the image from the day before next to it. Yesterday's image showed the infection had mostly been cleared up, while the abscess had not changed at all.

He then said, "I had you do two MRIs today because when I got the first one back, I thought there was a mistake." He then placed the second image they'd just taken beside the other images, and it looked vastly different. "It wasn't a mistake. You had the best Surgeon you could have had! Overnight, God fused your spine and removed the abscess. You don't need either surgery now. You should feel things in your legs you haven't felt in a while."

Jaci and I sat there, stunned. We looked at each other in shock, followed by tremendous relief and joy. She reminded me that I had woken up earlier that morning complaining of pain in my knees. I had said that without thinking about what it meant for me to have feeling in my legs. The doctor interjected that the pain I was starting to feel was from the nerves coming back alive. He added, "God actually blocked you from feeling pain in your legs during the illness." Obviously, God was in control the whole time.

I remember thinking about Psalm 23 from when I was a kid. How David is confident in his Shepherd, the Lord, even while facing life threatening danger. There are two lines that offered me hope that day and continue to, whenever I face moments of anxiety. The first line is, "for you are with me." We are not alone. No matter how deep the hole, or how silent and dark the night, we are not in this all by ourselves. We might not be able to see or sense Him, but God Almighty is right there with us. God was with me, it was undeniable.

The second line that stood out to me is, "even though I walk through the valley." The valley seems so lonely. God didn't lead me into the deep valley I had found myself in only to leave me there. He was leading me through it. And He carried me when I could no longer walk. He was with me in the entire valley, not waiting at the end, letting his voice echo down the ravine.

The Good News for each of us is that God is doing the same thing for everyone. It might not look like a miraculous removal of a fatal infection in your body (I still can't believe He did that for me), but it will be tangible, nonetheless. A Shepherd guides and protects, and He does so from close proximity. He doesn't stand at the end of the valley and hope His voice is loud enough to echo through the distance. He leads us through by walking, in my case carrying, and comforting us.

> "The Lord is my shepherd; I shall not want. He makes me lie down in green pastures. He leads me beside still waters. He restores my soul. He leads me in paths of righteousness for his name's sake. Even though *I walk through the valley* of the shadow of death, I will fear no evil, *for you are with me*; your rod and your staff they comfort me." (Psalm 23:1-4, ESV, emphasis added)

I am beyond thankful God chose to heal me. It is unbelievable what was, and what could have been, but isn't. I sit here writing, which is a big deal because I should be dead, but also because I can get up when I am done here and walk down the stairs and be a fairly normal husband and father with no barriers or complications. I say "fairly normal" because I am still a rascal, as wacky and zany as ever. My family would never let me get away with calling myself normal.

One of the best parts of how God led me through the valley is not that He saved me from the shadow of death, but that He led me so my family and friends could bear witness. The testimony below shows that in true colors.

Our daughter, Rachel, is a strong believer in the Lord as her Shepherd. I didn't realize how much she was observing when she was so young, but my ordeal deeply affected her. When she was in middle school, Rachel wrote a poem about her experience of observing my near-death condition, my feeling weak and unworthy, and my healing that occurred when she was five years old.

"Gateway to God" By Rachel Sharitz

As daily routines fade quickly away
I look at my dad in horror
His eyes, like death
His hopeless face
Nothing more I could say

Day after day and night after night
We pray and pray with tears of fright
Hoping and hoping
That maybe just maybe
My poor, weak dad will grasp hold of God

Trips to the doctor
Emergency rooms
My thoughts for my dad
Faith and doom

Through painful medicines
And heart-crushing back pains
My hopeless father surrenders to God

Many nights later, the light appeared
My dad was not leaving
But staying here.

I love this poem. I don't know how a middle schooler could have so much wisdom, but clearly the Holy Spirit helped her write this. She didn't just recall the details of horror and a hopeless face, but she saw God there with me. She was painfully aware of my resistance to grab hold of Him, and she watched me surrender to Him. While this was a great victory for me, it was a powerful experience for her to witness as well. It is the most important example I could model to my family—me trusting Jesus, surrendering to Him, and yielding control.

I think this is one of the hardest things for us to do, while at the same time, it is one of the most impactful things we can do. Certainly, there are societies that limit people's sense of individual control, but in our modern Western society we can usually get by reasonably well by taking control of things ourselves. Perhaps the Enemy has created a sense of self-sufficiency in us, but we probably did a good job working towards that all on our own. At least I know I did. The problem is that we aren't self-sufficient. We are Savior-sufficient, whether we know it or not. At our worst we're still good enough because of God's goodness. At our lowest point we can still be a bright light, the light of Jesus, for others. God can still use us to touch others when we think we have nothing to give.

Is there anyone alive who thinks they can walk through the valley of the shadow of death and successfully navigate it alone? I used to think there were people capable of walking through anything. These people had some sort of proverbial playbook that I didn't have yet, but if I worked hard enough, I would earn it or discover it. I just had to fake it until I could make it. I now know that isn't remotely true in any part of our lives, but especially when it comes to death. The saying that "death is the great equalizer" indicates to me that no matter how rich, powerful, influential, mighty, or any other attribute we might aspire to, it can't make us self-sufficient enough to beat death. All the control in the world won't stop that from happening to anyone.

For this reason, I am grateful for the awful season of pain and suffering that I experienced. Almost dying showed me I was barely living. It is remarkable how real our need for a Savior is. It's also remarkable how easy it is for us to assume we are truly self-sufficient. This is why I want so badly to share my story, because I know there are a bunch of other TJs out there who want (need) to be in control, falsely believing to be sufficient in their own abilities. I wish I could have heard and understood this narrative when I was younger. Better yet, I wish I could have read this book myself. Being as controlling and stubborn as I was, I probably still would have needed to go through it, but I have hope that others can learn the important lesson of surrender through me. If a hopeless man like me can surrender to God, maybe others also will learn to do so.

17

Stubborn Man's Attention

In the same way, let your light shine before others, so that they may see your good works and give glory to your Father who is in heaven. (Matthew 5:16, ESV)

AS MY CONDITION STARTED IMPROVING and I could use a walker, freedom was finally at hand. We became creative on ways I could join in on the kids' activities. Jaci packed a big blanket and pillows, along with all the kids' gear, got me into the car, and drove us to Rachel and Daniel's T-ball practices. She drove out onto the grass to get as close as possible to the field, so I didn't have far to walk. She'd help get me out of the car and pull out my walker, so I could navigate over to the dugout area. Jaci laid out the blankets and pillows on the ground next to the dugout. Even their coaches gave me a hand, helping me get down onto the ground. It meant so much to me that my family and the coaches would do that. I joked about how I decided to never try to walk on my own so I could keep getting this kind of posh luxury box treatment forever. I was like a little kid, laughing and cheering so hard for these kids. It was such a joy for me to be outside, even if only for a little while.

As I got stronger and began to shed the walker, all I wanted to do was to be out in the yard throwing footballs with the kids. It didn't matter to me that the lawn wasn't perfectly manicured. A neighbor of mine volunteered to cut the grass for me and he did a pretty good job. But let's be honest, the old controlling me would have had that lawn in meticulous shape.

That's not what mattered anymore.

I didn't need to control everything, especially the things that didn't really matter. I got to play my favorite sport with my kids in the yard again. *I got to play with my kids!* This was something to be grateful for. Daniel called me Mike Vick (former star QB for the Atlanta Falcons, and of course the Virginia Tech Hokies) because I threw left-handed just like him. I couldn't scramble like he could yet, but at least I was now outside playing our own "National Championship Super Bowl" with my daughter and son. I loved it so much.

With this newfound independence, it was finally time to get back to work. The previous 18 months had been devastating on our personal and corporate finances. Seemingly overnight, I had gone to bed financially secure and when I opened my eyes the next morning our money was gone. We had whittled down our checking, savings, and even our retirement and kids' college funds. My company was still alive as we never missed any payments to my employees, contractors, and vendors, but figuratively, the company also needed to learn how to walk again. I was able to keep a few employees around during my illness, but none of them seemed excited to be the *lucky ones* to still work at Sharitz Marketing.

I was excited about getting back to work, but if I am being honest, I was also nervous about it. Work had been a place of total control for me. I had dumped all my effort and energy into making the business successful. All I knew was micro-managing every single thing about work. Would I be able to come back a different person and a more balanced leader? I hoped I would be able to, but that muscle memory was going to be hard to break.

On my first day back into the office, I intended to sit down one-on-one with every employee to thank them for their efforts to keep the business alive. Within a couple minutes of sitting down at my desk, I was told that someone had arrived who wanted to speak with me. Intrigued about who might be welcoming me back, maybe with an edible arrangement or joke wheelchair to get around the office, I ran right up to the front door. I didn't recognize the guy, so I was either confused or let down. He stated my name and handed me an envelope. This dude served me with papers informing me that my business was being sued by a former client. Talk about being kicked when you are down. I was so embarrassed as I walked back to my desk past my employees.

I spent the next hour on the phone trying to figure out what was going on. It was maddening to sit on hold forever and barely get any answers or clarity from anyone. Finally, I got a call back from my lawyer who was able to dig up some understanding. The client was suing us to get out of paying what they owed us. This wasn't as scary as I'd feared. I was disappointed to lose that revenue, but I certainly wasn't going to pay court fees and lawyer bills to potentially not get paid. So, I decided to write off their balance due and do my best to trust that God had a future for my little company.

Jaci called me shortly thereafter to remind me that I could only stay at work for a couple of hours, as I still needed to rest and ease my way into things. I didn't fight it, so I packed up, telling everyone as I left, I would do their one-on-ones the next day. While I was driving back home, it started to rain really hard. I was thankful to have new tires on my car this time, but of course, I got another flat tire. I pulled over into a parking lot and got out of my car to see the damage. I had somehow run over a large piece of metal debris. It had blown out the same rear tire as had happened a few months earlier when it had rained this hard on the way to the hospital.

I caught myself from throwing a fit in the parking lot, opting to laugh instead and say, "Okay God, you really have my attention this time. Stop the rain and I'll take my family back to church this coming Sunday." *Wouldn't you know it*, the rain stopped. I simply nodded my head with acceptance, changed the tire, and announced that we would be attending Duluth United Methodist Church the following weekend. That Sunday's message? "Jesus heals the Crippled Man." I wish I was making this stuff up. God knows how to get a stubborn man's attention for sure.

Since it had been a long time since any of us had gone to church, we weren't totally sure how to jump in. We didn't initiate many conversations and felt a little out of place, but I had made a commitment, so we were going to see this through. We filled out a visitors' card without much understanding of what that would do for us. Perhaps we would get flyers in the mail about bake sales and whatnot.

A few days later, an old childhood friend stopped by to say hello and welcome us to his church. He had been at the Methodist Church on Sunday, had noticed our visitors' card, and wanted to be the one to reach out to us.

I'm not sure I would have recognized him if we had bumped into each other at church, but it was good to see him. We caught up for a while and shared our stories, which led perfectly into why we had visited the church. I was authentic with him about all my control issues, sharing how God had shown up in absurd ways.

My old friend listened attentively. When I was done sharing my story, he said, "Wow, TJ, I am so glad you shared that with me. It is a very powerful story." I assumed he was being overly courteous with his words, but he seemed sincere about it. I was kind of taken aback when he struggled to find words to reply. It seemed like maybe he was about to cry.

"Your story reminds me so much of Peter, one of Jesus' disciples. He had so much vigor and energy to win, but often it was misguided. Peter's story speaks to me because it tells me that I don't have to try so hard; I have to *trust* so hard. When Peter chooses to trust Jesus, everything changes. I see everything changing in your life because you are choosing to trust Jesus as well."

Yeah, I get Peter. We're old buds.

For the first time, I started to think of myself in a different way. Not as someone who stubbornly works hard to get his way and overcome (this was one of my favorite attributes about myself), but as an actual disciple of Jesus. God had led me through the fire where I lost everything I thought was important and discovered all I truly needed was Him. As a disciple, my story matters. Not just to church veterans, like my friend in our living room, but to anyone and possibly everyone.

I suppose this is the first time I thought of writing this book. Not that I ever saw myself as an author (especially knowing how hard that is for non-dyslexics), but I realized that God wanted me to not be ashamed. He knew it would be hard work to share my story of yielding control to Him. Following my old patterns, I started to feel like I needed to share my story with everyone, right now! I began to think of all the ways I could creatively share my story with people. I got lost in dreaming about the major motion picture and who was going to play me (Matthew McConaughey or Brad Pitt? It's so hard to choose). And then I realized … *I don't need to control this*. I just need to keep my eyes and ears open for the opportunities that God has for me to share my story with His people. Of course, writing this book is one of those opportunities, and I've been letting the Lord guide the entire process. None of it has gone as easily as I would have hoped. But it is a chance to trust so hard, just like Peter.

18

Dyslexia is Not a Curse

And we know that God causes everything to work together for the good of those who love God and are called according to his purpose for them. (Romans 8:28, NLT)

A **FEW YEARS AFTER MY ILLNESS** and recovery, our son Daniel started learning to read. I was personally super excited about him reading because that meant I would have to read less on his behalf. When he would ask me what a billboard said as we drove past, I would immediately start to sweat because I knew there was a good chance, I was either going to get it wrong or just lie and make up something to save face. I required more time than four seconds to decipher what things said, but he didn't know that.

As he started to verbalize his reading, Jaci noticed differences in how he read compared to Rachel. By the end of first grade, Jaci voiced her concerns to Daniel's teacher. She told Jaci not to worry because boys and girls develop these kinds of skills at unequal speeds. I told her the same thing. By the end of second grade, her "Momma's intuition" was heightened with certainty that things weren't right. She went to the teacher whom Rachel had for third grade and said if she could figure out a way to get Daniel in her class, Jaci would be her room mom for the year. The teacher was happy to accommodate this request.

During Daniel's third grade year, Jaci and the teacher began to work together to figure out why he was struggling with reading and comprehension. One day when they were reviewing his homework, they discovered his short story summary reflected nothing about the story. Trying to understand where he was getting his comprehension from, Jaci noticed that his summary told an imagined story based on guessing what the pictures in the book meant. When asked about it, Daniel admitted that he never read any of the words, but instead just looked at the pictures. This had tricked a lot of teachers up through second grade, but the books they were reading now in third grade had fewer pictures, and the pictures were no longer concrete to the story line. Finally, we knew our son had a reading problem. His wonderful teacher went to bat with the administration to get him tested.

The testing quickly revealed that Daniel had a "learning difference." His IQ scores were much higher when measured with puzzles or numbers than when he was quizzed with word problems. I was crushed.

I had passed my dyslexia on to my son.

The public school system used the term "learning difference" because they didn't want to label him negatively. *My, how times had changed from when I was in school.* Jaci and I were insistent on getting it officially diagnosed as dyslexia or whatever he was struggling with, so we could find him the help he needed. We talked with the school system psychiatrist, asking her directly if we should look for programs to help kids with dyslexia.

She nodded a silent Yes.

We hired a neighbor who was a teacher to work with Daniel one-on-one to improve his reading and comprehension. We also sent him to a two-week reading workshop at the Schenck School, which specializes in helping dyslexic children. I loved what we were doing to try to help Daniel. It was obviously very personal to me that we gave him all the resources possible and that he felt supported by us. Of course, there is no roadmap for how to properly help someone with a problem like dyslexia. What works for one kid might not help the next. All I knew was that I didn't want him becoming a total control freak like me.

As Daniel started fourth grade, Jaci shared her concerns with me about public school not being able to truly help him. She pointed out that his "old soul" spirit was slowly being torn down by his struggles with reading and, more specifically, the understanding of what he was reading. He could no longer rely on pictures to help him guess what the words were communicating. She told me she had looked at several different schools that offered programs for dyslexic kids. Unfortunately, none of the schools seemed to be a good fit for Daniel. She seemed broken hearted about how hard this was. Then, she said she was going to head to the grocery store to give her some time to think more about this dilemma.

After a couple of hours, she returned home and came straight to my office. She was excited and had a great big smile. "While I was shopping, I ran into a childhood friend of mine," she said. "I shared with her Daniel's struggles and our unsuccessful search for programs to help him with his dyslexia. She said that their oldest son also had dyslexia and had just graduated from the Woodward Academy with honors after going through their unique transition program. She gave me the name of the director, Selma Ridgway, and her phone number. I am going to call her first thing tomorrow morning." This was another miracle for us and a big answer to prayer. I felt hopeful that my son wouldn't have to struggle like I did.

The next morning, Jaci called Mrs. Ridgway and shared Daniel's struggles along with what we had been doing to try to help him. They set up an appointment to meet at Woodward's main campus the following morning. When we arrived at the school, Selma took Daniel into her office alone where he could read and then share what he had read. After a few minutes, she opened the door and informed us that she agreed with the dyslexia diagnosis. She also said she was very concerned about how far behind he had fallen academically. She feared he was reading below a first-grade level, despite being in the fourth grade. He needed to be pulled out of public school immediately and placed into their transition program as soon as possible if we hoped he would recover and succeed in school. This stirred up a lot of emotions in me. I felt pain as I recalled what it was like to repeat third grade and go to a new school where I knew no one.

On top of the regular tuition, we also needed to pay the extra "transition" tuition and fees for him to have two professional therapists for the entire year. All of this needed to be paid up front, along with buying him a new laptop computer and school uniform. We agreed and paid on the spot for him to start the very next day.

Predictably, Daniel was not exactly on board with leaving his friends and moving to a new school. He didn't want to use an "awful laptop" or wear a "stupid uniform." I did my best to explain how this would help him in the long run, that I was jealous he had this opportunity because programs like this didn't exist when I was a kid. My parents did their very best to help me, but there just weren't resources like this out there. I assured him the changes and challenges were all going to be worth it.

The next morning, I drove Daniel to the campus. We walked together into his new classroom where he met his new teacher and classmates. The transition class was much smaller than the usual 20-plus students in the public-school classroom. All six kids in the lass were excited to meet Daniel. Each wanted Daniel to sit next to him or her. There was already a Daniel in this class, so our Daniel became DJ, which he thought sounded pretty cool. A kid named Charlie came up to him and asked DJ if he knew how to set up his laptop. When Daniel admitted he didn't have a clue how to do it, Charlie sat next to him and made it happen. The rest of the class affirmed that Charlie was the class computer guru and DJ should definitely sit with him. I watched my son's disposition change from fearful to enthusiastic about this new experience. I left that classroom and could not wait to call Jaci to let her know how well drop-off had gone and how great of a fit this all seemed to be. I was so excited and proud it was hard to keep the tears in.

That afternoon, I drove back and nervously waited in the parent pickup line for the bell to ring. DJ's teacher escorted him out to my car. I began to brace for the impact that maybe the day didn't go so well after all. To the contrary, she wanted to tell me just how great things went and how the whole class couldn't wait to see him again in the morning. What a relief!

On the drive home, Daniel asked me if he could use my cell phone. This was an odd request, but I handed it to him without much thought. Then I heard him say, "Nana, this is Daniel. I just want to thank you for my dad, and what you and Grandpa Charlie did for him when you discovered he had dyslexia. He is the dad he is because of what you did for him. He and Mommy are doing so much to help me so I can overcome it like he did."

Are you kidding me?

I began to cry as I listened to my son show his gratitude. He was handling these struggles and changes with grace and a joyful heart. His words pierced my heart. He was teaching me to be a better person and a better parent. I realized that my dyslexia was not a curse, but an honest-to-goodness gift from God. He knew DJ would have this struggle, just like me. God used the tough times I had as a child to prepare me for this very moment with my own son. To be honest, I admit I was jealous that the support afforded to him made it possible for DJ to feel joy and gratitude. Unlike me, he was more like Paul in the Bible, who even while in prison, found a grateful heart. I know this sounds petty, but it would have been easier to not assume control in everything if other people had known, understood, cared, and had a plan about how to handle dyslexia when I was a kid. I had to sit with this thought for a bit before I was able to kick it to the curb. I had to process it and realize that we don't have control of anything in this life, outside of our response. Regardless of the circumstances, I am responsible for my responses. My son had chosen the right response, while I hadn't. To say it clearly: I am very proud of my son for choosing such a good response to a hard situation.

Although Rachel doesn't have dyslexia, we made the decision to move her out of public school and into Woodward as well. This was a good move for her, but we weren't living very close to the school, which required the kids to be stuck on a bus for two hours every day. So, we found a beautiful old home, built in the 1920s, closer to the school in the Historic College Park area south of Atlanta. We moved there in 2008.

In the months leading up to the move, we prayed so hard that our other home would sell fast, but it didn't. Shortly after we made the move, I got an email asking for prayers for a young family whose house had recently burned down. The mother and her three teenage kids had been living in a motel room for the past couple of weeks, and on that day they had to move out with nowhere to go. It just so happened that these kids were in the same school that DJ and Rachel used to go to in Duluth. I got up from my desk and went to find Jaci to see if she thought we could help this family. Jaci met me on the stairs. She was coming to find me about the same email.

We immediately contacted the school principal, offering our home to the family in need. Fortunately, our home was a great fit for them, including being right down the road from their school. They moved in that afternoon. This was such a joyful experience for both us and them. We weren't looking for compensation; we just wanted to help them out while we had the opportunity with a second home. The family's insurance company ended up paying us rent, which was more than enough to cover our mortgage and expenses. This was a blessing for us because the housing market had completely bottomed out during this time. We have no idea how long we would have sat on that house and struggled to pay two mortgages.

The months renting our home allowed me extra time to put together a Facebook site with pictures and details that showcased our home effectively. On the day the family that was renting our house moved out, I posted the page and got a lot of likes on it in short order. Within minutes, someone reached out saying they were very interested in the house. They wanted to see it that afternoon. As chance would have it, I had been working in Duluth that day, so I could be there quickly. When I arrived at the house, the couple was already there, watching their boys throw a football around on the yard, which was perfectly manicured, of course, in National Championship Super Bowl style. As I walked over to the couple, the wife had tears in her eyes. She told me they had been praying the previous night for God to bless them with a new home. More specifically, a home on a cul-de-sac with a big backyard where the boys could safely play. They had been looking for a long time and were convinced our house was a direct answer to their prayers. This family purchased our home and moved in right away.

All of this seemed like enough proof that God could be trusted with the hardest of circumstances. This strengthened my desire to continue yielding control to Him, but I can't say it was easy. The year 2008 was incredibly challenging for all Americans financially. My business took a major hit during this time. We went from having over 200 active and profitable clients to a small handful of barely active clients. To make matters even worse, the clients we lost went bankrupt or sold their businesses off with little or no profit. Thus, we lost most of our income receivables from clients who couldn't pay us. In the blink of an eye, our profitable business fell $300,000 in debt.

There is a beautiful verse in Mark where a man tells Jesus that he believes but asks for help with his unbelief (Mark 9:24). I mutter these words to myself often, but what is unique about this verse is that this man is literally in front of Jesus asking for him to heal his son. Why in the world would he be in front of Jesus if he didn't believe? I just can't understand this. The guy had so much faith that he went to Jesus' disciples first. Perhaps this simply shows desperation, but maybe it shows something else. I think he is saying that he believes right in that moment, but he is being honest that in the future, he knows he's going to struggle to believe. We all have a propensity for anxiety or worry about the future.

Jaci and I had belief that things with the house would turn out fine. We should have been panicked, but we knew we were doing the right thing by moving close to the Woodward school. This was important for our kids, and we prayed it through. While we didn't get a burning bush kind of response, we did feel like God was pushing us in the direction of buying the College Park house. But it is always hard to decipher if that is truly God or if it is simply me trying to convince myself. We made the move with the simple belief that He was in it. But that usually doesn't translate into future belief. Just look at my story, I constantly take back control because somehow, *I know better.*

True belief requires consistency. That might seem too obvious or too bold, but I think it's true. With my company tanking right in front of me, and my consistency of being inconsistent, I wanted to freak out and take control in 18,000 different ways. But I just let it all happen, continuing to ask the Lord to help my unbelief. This stuff ain't easy. Our humanity is just too real. Fortunately, these experiences are opportunities to learn, and I still had more to learn.

19

Swag, Not Swagger

Have I not commanded you? Be strong and courageous. Do not be terrified; do not be discouraged, for the Lord your God will be with you wherever you go. (Joshua 1:9, NIV)

AT HIS NEW SCHOOL, DJ was given an assignment to memorize the Jabberwocky poem from *Alice in Wonderland.* A bunch of nonsensical, hard-to-pronounce words. This was now personal, squarely hitting a lot of different wounds from my school days. I was angry. We were paying all this money for a special educational program, only to have them assign something that a dyslexic child could not do.

Jaci was concerned too and scheduled a conference with his teacher, Ms. Dunbar. Jaci suggested she should take the lead on this since it was so personal for me, and when we spoke with her, we both expressed our disbelief and concern about such an inappropriate assignment.

Ms. Dunbar turned and looked directly at us and said, "You'll be amazed at what DJ can do when you get out of his way."

WOW! Talk about speaking truth! Okay, that hurt.

Then it hit me. I was doing exactly that. Unintentionally, I was passing my pains and limitations on to my son while trying to keep control. Jaci, on the other hand, thought she was protecting our son, but instead she was placing limits on DJ without even realizing it. Those words were so powerful and true for both Jaci and me. From that moment forward, we trusted the guidance that God led us to for DJ. DJ worked all evening with Jaci on the poem. By the next morning, he had not only memorized the poem, he acted it out with great emotions and animation.

When I got out of DJ's way, he did great. But could I get out of my own way?

As my business continued to collapse, I did my best to trust God with our future. DJ started to pick up on the fact that things might not be going well at work. One day in the car, he randomly blurted out from the backseat, "Dad, don't worry about your business. This time you have your health. You will be okay. God's got this."

His young, yet bold, faith made me smile, giving me reassurance that I was on the right path. All that really mattered is that I was passing along a legacy of faith to my family. My business could go away, and everything would be fine knowing that my kids wouldn't be deterred from trusting the Lord. Daniel had once again reminded me—Mr. Hardheaded Meathead—to have faith and not worry because God was with me.

Later that same week, one of Woodward Academy's assistant athletic directors asked me to come help them coach their kickers. Since I didn't have much business at the time, I agreed to help them out. After a few weeks of coaching, the kickers showed a great deal of improvement, so the school signed me to a coaching contract.

I also began to get asked to substitute teach at Woodward. I was now coaching year-round, including swimming and lacrosse, and was readily available to the school. I never considered coaching or teaching as a supplement to my income, but I started to enjoy these opportunities. All I needed to do was the thing DJ suggested from the back seat of the car—trust that God had this.

> "Have I not commanded you? Be strong and courageous. Do not be afraid; do not be discouraged, for the Lord your God will be with you wherever you go." (Joshua 1:9, ESV)

This encouragement was something I was able to give back to DJ a while later as he was finishing seventh grade. He had overcome many of the obstacles dyslexia gave him, and it was clear he was ready to slide over to mainstream school. But he was the youngest in his class, and the transition administrator felt he would benefit from an extra year to mature mentally before he entered high school. She recommended an extended eighth grade—two years instead of one—with extra learning opportunities. Now was the best time to give him an extra year.

We sat down with DJ and explained why we thought this was the best decision for him. Personally, I was having severe flashbacks to the time my parents told me I would have to repeat third grade.

It mortified me to do this to my own son, especially so late, with him now going into eighth grade, but I knew it would help him out a bunch. Did he respond like I did years ago, trying to talk us out of this horrible decision? Nope, he was totally cool with it. How is this remarkable young man my son? We're so much alike, yet totally different. I'm shortsighted, guarded, and emotional. DJ, on the other hand, is all trusting, faithful, senses the moment, and reacts like an old soul. His only condition for doing two years of eighth grade was for him to be able to attend a different school with different kids who didn't know he was repeating a year. We thought this was a tremendous idea and agreed.

Later, I took him on a walk with the intention of reaffirming him, and mostly myself on this hard decision, but I barely got a word out when he said, "Dad, if you and Mom think this is a good move for me, then I'm all for it. You don't have to worry about it. I'm great with it." I just about threw a parade right there on the sidewalk with my son. I don't even know what that would look like, but my pride was overflowing. I maybe should have rung every single doorbell along our route and told people they needed to grab a bowl of candy and get outside immediately because a parade of one incredibly wise kid was coming through. Instead, I kept this parade in my head, thanking God for what He was teaching DJ through my life and old stories. I was also growing from DJ's reactions and words. DJ had shot a torpedo of gratitude and sunk all worry.

During this time, I had several men who began to encourage me to read with intention. Not to read just anything, but to read books that would encourage, inspire, and bless my world. I started with *A Leadership Revolution* by Orrin Woodward. Orrin's words cut deep into my heart and inspired me to become a true leader. I became inspired to read a book a month. For my dyslexic brain, it helped getting physical books to read so I could highlight nuggets to remember, and at the same time listen along to the audio version. My entire world started to open as I learned to be a new leader in the family. More importantly, a servant leader.

That next fall, DJ began attending Landmark Christian School for eighth grade. We encouraged him to join the football team so he could meet some of the boys in his class. When I picked him up from his first practice, he was so excited to tell me all about his new friends and cool coaches. He immediately told me that he didn't want to go back to Woodward next year. He wanted to stay at Landmark because none of the coaches yelled or cussed at the boys. Plus, they created play calls using the names of different books of the Bible. I realized in that moment that one of DJ's love languages was words of affirmation and Landmark would probably be best for him at this stage. This seemed like a reasonable request and a great opportunity for him to grow in new and more important ways. I can admit that I was a little sad to miss the chance to coach him at Woodward, but I knew that God was in control. I didn't think twice about it.

As DJ continued his years at Landmark, his passion turned into playing basketball on a team with his friends. My son is a very good basketball player. As he grew up, he learned how to focus and be disciplined in learning how to shoot. It reminded me of the determination I showed in my effort to control things and (nearly) become a professional athlete. DJ's determination wasn't about control though, he truly enjoyed the sport, especially the friendships and camaraderie.

Their varsity basketball teams made the state tournament three of the four years he played. The ball players were like a super close family. They had each other's backs, always encouraging and pushing each other to do their best.

One day after one of their big basketball wins, DJ asked me, "Dad, what do you think gives me swag?"

I was quick to reply. "You get your swagger from hitting a game winning deep-three at the buzzer."

"Really, Dad? It's swag, not swagger. And no that's not it."

I thought for a moment and then said, "It's when you get the ball and pass it to a teammate for them to hit an open shot."

"No, Dad, none of that gives me swag." Then with a big smile he says, "You give me swag, Dad. Even with your dyslexia and struggles reading, you continue to read and listen to books to grow, improve yourself, and bless your relationship with Mom. You give me swag, Dad." *Wow.*

DJ was referring to my own personal leadership mentoring that, just a few years earlier, had encouraged me to read actual books and listen to audiobooks daily. Books and audios that I would then share with him, his sister, and Jaci. Tommy Newberry's book *The 4:8 Principle: The Secret to a Joy-Filled Life* helped me to change the lens with which I view the world, to have a grateful and joyful heart. Again, my own son was giving me words of wisdom from his own joy-filled heart. He always sees the good in people even when they're struggling, especially me.

My business slowly recovered from the recession, and I continued to coach varsity sports at Woodward while substitute teaching on occasion. As a coach, I had access to Woodward's indoor pool, where I would swim most mornings with other teachers and coaches. The water has always been a place of peace and rejuvenation for me, and I was grateful this pool was so close and accessible.

During the fall of 2012, Woodward's pool had closed for two weeks for repairs. Once it reopened, I quickly jumped back in. During my warmup laps, I noticed something strange in my chest—there was no pain, pressure, or real discomfort. I don't exactly know how to describe it other than it felt like a chest hair or two were out of place. I know that's weird, but I was so distracted by it. Fortunately, the sensation went away as I got into the bulk of my swimming workout.

Two days later, the same thing happened as I was warming up in the pool again. I mentioned this to Jaci, and we agreed I needed to schedule a physical, especially since my dad died at the age of 52 from a heart attack and I was now 52. I wasn't as worried about it as Jaci was, but I was concerned enough that I didn't drag my feet at calling the doctor to get a physical on the calendar. The nurse told me she had just gotten a cancellation for a physical for the following day, so I could jump right into that open slot.

After the physical, the doctor had me do an EKG. That test showed no signs of heart issues or trauma, but he still seemed concerned so he decided to order a stress test that we could use as a benchmark moving forward. He gave me the phone number to a cardiologist so I could schedule an appointment as soon as possible. I called the cardiologist on the drive home and, as crazy as it sounds, the scheduler said she had just gotten off the phone with someone who needed to cancel the following day. This put me on notice. God must have been coordinating something unique here.

That next day, I sat down with the cardiologist. He wanted to check me out and understand my medical history before putting me through the stress test. He agreed that I should get a stress test done, but there was nothing indicating a need to expedite the test, so he told me to speak with the scheduler about getting on the calendar in about two months. I had no concept what my schedule would look like that far out, so I promised the scheduler I would call her when I could see my full work calendar.

As I was getting into my car, I heard a lady calling my name, "Mr. Sharitz, Mr. Sharitz!" I jumped out of my car, thinking I had forgotten something or there was an emergency. She said, "We just got a cancellation for a stress test tomorrow morning. Would you be able to take that appointment?" I didn't care what I had going on the next day. I knew I needed to make this happen.

The stress test seemed to go fine from my perspective. I got a call that afternoon from the cardiologist while I was coaching swimming, and he told me I had done very well on the test, especially for someone 52 years old. However, there were some abnormalities that he wanted to look at a little closer. He assured me there was nothing to worry about, but he recommended a heart cath to rule out any serious issues. This procedure runs a wire through an artery in the wrist or thigh up into the coronary arteries in the heart where they shoot dye through the blood vessels to identify any blockages. I immediately asked him what time the following day I could do this heart cath. He told me that he appreciated my gusto, but I would have to wait until the following week. I told him I would be patient, even though it made for a better story if I could immediately get in.

The following week, Jaci took me to the hospital, where we met my mom so Jaci wouldn't have to sit and wait all alone. I was thankful Mom was there for Jaci, especially when the doctor came out to announce to her that my "widow maker" was 99 percent blocked and they had to put a stent in my heart. If that last 1 percent would have gotten blocked, I almost certainly would have died without immediate emergency care. In fact, the cardiologist informed us he considered it a miracle I did not have a catastrophic event in the week leading up to this appointment. No wonder God was giving me countless "warp zones" to arrange next day appointments when everything should have taken weeks or months. My somewhat healthy lifestyle and strong heart had fooled the stress test, but divine coordination (something I could not control in my wildest dreams) saved me once again.

As I was about to go under, the surgeon had asked me what type of music I wanted to listen to during the procedure. I replied, Rock-N-Roll! When he woke me after the heart cath, Led Zeppelin's "Stairway to Heaven" was playing. God even used music to make good news more impactful.

It makes me think of a story found in John 9, where Jesus and the disciples stumble upon a man who was blind his entire life. The disciples ask Jesus whose sin caused him to be blind, his or his parents? I imagine Jesus shook his head to communicate just how far off they were with their thinking. He told them it had nothing to do with sin and everything to do with seeing the power of God on display through this man. Jesus then healed his blindness.

Could you imagine being this man seeing the world for the first time? If I were him, I wonder what I would want to do first. Probably run to see my family for the first time. Well, this man opted to run into town and tell people what just happened to him. Of course, no one believed him, and he has to reiterate his story multiple times, saying, "Once I was blind, but now I can see." What a powerful story! It's a simple story that carries so much weight. This story probably brought so many people into a place where they were willing to consider the reality of who Jesus is. This is all I want for my life.

I probably should have run into town and told people right away when this event happened to me. I should have written this book sooner and shared the story that puts the power of God on display for everyone to see. I know it's okay that I didn't, but I am so glad to be able to do it now. The lesson I have learned in all this is that we all must share our stories while we have a chance.

20

Door Holder

Having gifts that differ according to the grace given to us, let us use them.... (Romans 12:6, ESV)

WHILE DJ WAS IN HIGH school, he began playing basketball on AAU travel squads, which took us all over Atlanta to watch him play in tournaments nearly every weekend. The full schedule made it difficult for us to attend church together as a family regularly. I began watching sermons on video whenever I could, my favorite being Andy Stanley's recorded messages that aired after Saturday Night Live (recorded, of course; I couldn't stay up that late!). It was there that I learned about Andy's childhood friend, Louie Giglio, and his church, Passion City. Both were local pastors in the metro Atlanta area, with Louie's church just a few miles north of our home.

I knew I should be doing more to foster a relationship with God and His people for my kids during that time, but it was honestly such a challenge juggling their sports and activities on top of everything I was trying to do. Fortunately, my kids were self-starters when it came to developing a faith community.

One afternoon during DJ's senior year, he came into my home

office and asked if he could attend the three-day Passion Conference at the Georgia Dome with his coach and teammates. I wasn't totally sure what the Passion Conference was, but I assumed it had to do with the church somehow. I obviously said yes to this request, and it turned out to be a great experience for him.

When DJ headed off to college, and Rachel was by then in her junior year of college, Jaci and I were suddenly empty nesters. It was such a weird season of having a much more open calendar and a quiet home. Jaci approached me one day and suggested that since we were empty nesters, we should start going to church again. "I would like you to step up and be our spiritual leader. Go find a church that will fill you up spiritually, and that will be our church."

What a challenge! As much as I would have preferred doing this with her, I like that she gave me the responsibility and trusted me to choose. Also, she worked at the pharmacy every other weekend, so it made sense for me to find the church that would equip me to lead.

The first place I wanted to check out was Passion City Church. It absolutely blew me away how powerful the worship "gathering" (the name PCC calls services) was. On top of the amazing message from Louie, the production value spoke to this video guy's heart! The production team was so professional, paying incredible attention to detail and creativity. After the gathering, I walked to the back of the room and met the producer and several audio people. I wanted to join their team. I knew I could hang with their technical abilities, but they didn't know me, so I wasn't sure how I would be received. They were very friendly and enthusiastic, telling me to visit the church's website. The producer told me to click on the "Door Holder" tab to sign up for the video production team. When I made a face over the "Door Holder" thing, she laughed. I wasn't the first person to be confused by that term. She explained that a Door Holder is someone who serves with pleasure in opening a way for others to see and experience Jesus. They do not call them volunteers—volunteers can lack ownership and commitment. Door Holders are the very heartbeat of Passion City Church. I thought this was one of the most inspiring things I had ever heard. I pulled out my phone and filled out the form right there before I left the building, even sending them my professional resume.

They called me the very next day, asking me to come in for training the following Sunday. I ended up serving on two different teams as a camera operator for worship gatherings and special video projects. If I was going to be at church every Sunday, why not serve and get to hear the message two or three times? I needed that many times to let it soak into my soul. Jaci was always impressed by my recall of verses and applications from the sermons when she wasn't there. I decided to take the whole "spiritual leadership" thing seriously.

I was asked to run camera at the Passion Conference over New Year's week in 2016. I jumped at the opportunity to be back on camera at such a huge venue, especially at the Georgia Dome where the Atlanta Falcons play football. Whenever I drove by the stadium, I'd tell myself how cool it would have been to still be in the league when it opened and get to kick in such an amazing arena. That was an old broken dream, but working this conference there felt somehow just as important and fulfilling, if not even more.

The following year, at Passion 2017, I served as a dolly grip for one of the cameras on the Georgia Dome floor. I know "dolly grip" sounds like a moderately inappropriate position to serve. But honestly, it's an incredibly fun job. I got to push a giant dolly cart with a video camera and a camera operator back and forth along a track. This camera provided shots that created incredible energy and intimate moments for the director to use on the massive LED screens hanging inside the dome.

During one of our breaks, I noticed a small lighted stage close to the dolly track where a group of women performed sign language for the hearing-impaired section at the conference. I walked over there and introduced myself to them. It immediately got weird when I asked if any of them could speak because I did not know sign language. They all laughed, explaining they had to be good at both spoken and sign language since they were interpreters. That made sense. I pushed past my embarrassment to ask if they wanted to hear a cool Jesus signing story. They enthusiastically said yes, simultaneously signing both what I said and what they said. That threw me off slightly. I told them that they didn't need to sign it for me since I didn't know the language. They assured me that it was just a habit for them, so I did my best to not be distracted by it.

The story basically goes like this: One of my best friends from high school, on his very first day on campus at the University of

Georgia, noticed a beautiful blonde girl in line while registering for classes. It was love at first sight. He noticed that she was signing, so he decided right then and there to use one of his electives to register for a sign language class so he could impress her with his signing skills when he met her.

He ended up loving the class so much that he changed his major to become a professional sign language interpreter. After graduation, he got a job with the Atlanta Hawks, who had just drafted the first non-hearing NBA player. He spent the next several years working with this player as he went from team to team, as well as helping him set up basketball camps for non-hearing children.

The ladies interrupted me, "What about the girl? Does he ever get the girl?" I clearly disappointed this group when I told them that he didn't. I am certain one of the women signed "This is the stupidest Jesus story about sign language I've ever heard."

I pressed on and told the rest of the story.

Years down the road, he finally met his wife, and God blessed them with a son. Shortly after his birth, they discovered that he had cerebral palsy and would never be able to hear. God had prepared him ahead of time to be able to communicate with his son. Just like God had done for me and my son.

As I finished the story, I saw the students in the non-hearing section crying and shaking their hands, the sign language equivalent of applause. It hadn't occurred to me that the students sitting up in that section had also experienced the story. They got to learn about my friend's story thanks to the interpreters doing what they do best.

I'd only intended to share this Jesus story with the few, but God wanted all the students to discover His great news.

Six months later, I got a call from my old friend the interpreter who asked me if I was a part of the Passion Conference. That was an oddly specific question, but when I told him that I was, he said he knew it was me who shared his story. Apparently, my friend was attending an international sign language conference and heard one of the guest speakers sharing this sweet Jesus signing story from the Passion Conference that she had heard from one of her college students. I was totally blown away! Our God is so much bigger than we can imagine. My thinking is so, so small, being content with sharing God's story with a few people. God took this story and blessed thousands. God is that big. This story made the rounds and undoubtedly communicated something important about God: that He knows, and He cares. The same way that God prepared me to be able to help DJ with dyslexia, God prepared my friend because He knew what was coming with his son, and he cared.

This truth about God is exactly what I and my fellow Door Holders want people to see and experience. The job to show God's love belongs to us—all believers, not exclusively Passion City Church people—putting the power of God on display for others to see.

The greatest example I can think of from the Bible about people Door Holding is found in Mark 2. Jesus was sitting in a house jam packed full of people. There are four men who have decided to care for a paralytic man, and they know they need to get this man, who is trapped on a mat, in front of Jesus, by any means possible. No one was holding the door for them. Even if someone had been at the door, there was no room to move this man through the house. So, they literally cut a hole in the roof and lowered this man and his mat down to Jesus. It's an incredible story.

The best part about this story is that Jesus knew, and He cared. He wasn't surprised, concerned, worried, startled, or confused that a human being was essentially falling on him. There was a barrier between Him and this paralyzed man, and I believe Jesus doesn't like barriers between us and Him. Barriers like closed doors. We must be Door Holders for people. And sometimes we even need to be Roof Cutters for people. Jesus knows, and He cares, and we can take away the barriers that exist.

For me, I let my need for control and winning be the thing that caused a barrier between me and Him. I don't know what barriers you struggle with, but when the barrier is eliminated between you and Jesus, you become a Door Holder and Roof Cutter who can do the same thing for others. This pumps me up. I don't know who all was deeply encouraged by the sign language story, but I know that a story like that can remove barriers of disbelief for people. That's the power of God on display!

21

I'm Not Okay, but Jesus Is

Submit yourselves, then, to God. Resist the devil, and he will flee from you. (James 4:7, NIV)

PASTOR LOUIE HAD RECENTLY TAKEN the church through the book of James. The first message of this series was called, "I'm Not Okay … but Jesus is." This sermon spoke to me in immense ways. Fortunately, he gave it on a day that I was running camera and got to hear it several times. His words reminded me that I should embrace with grace and give thanks for the trials, discomfort, and pains that come in life. We can do this because Jesus understands our pain and suffering as He suffered great pain and came through it victorious. We should pray for God not to take away our pain, but for our pain to be used for His good and glorious purposes. Thus, we should be of a joyful heart and not dwell in the muck or pain, but we should rejoice. As absurd as that sounded, rejoicing was completely foreign to me, especially in the midst of suffering.

As this series started, I faced some tough career decisions that would pull me in different directions. A good friend of mine strongly recommended I eliminate one of the options to ease the stress. As a result, I decided to end my high school coaching career at Woodward wonderful years. I felt an immediate release of stress, making ɛr to focus on the remaining two opportunities: Director of ĸeting for WinShape Marriage or production work with NBA TV network. This was risky, quitting the job I had been blessed to have while my marketing business struggled for the prospect of two others, but I felt bold at the time, obviously not as risk adverse as I possibly should have been.

Jaci and I prayed diligently that God would make His plan clear to us, and in short order, He did. WinShape notified me they had hired someone else, leaving me with one opportunity.

As things with NBA TV progressed, I invested myself into as much as I could at Passion City because I had the time. I also started to experience more back pain during this time. Not constant like my bone infection, just whenever I tried to walk. Every single day, the pain grew worse. As my back pain intensified, my mobility became more limited and I began adopting horrible eating habits again, which led me to gain 30 pounds. Don't believe the TV commercials. Eating king-sized Snickers bars doesn't make you feel like your old self, just a fatter self with more inflammation and discomfort. Not much joy there. This wasn't awesome for me, but I didn't have the gusto to turn things around very quickly.

A friend of mine introduced me to a "bed of nails" product designed to help increase blood flow and reduce back pain. It was literally a pad that had some 8,000+ pointed spikes on it. It helped a ton, despite how scary it was to lie down on. This thing was not comfortable, to say the least, but it worked. Talk about a real Scriptural lesson here—the more pain I endured, the more joy and hope I ended up with on the other side. I was very thankful that this torture device was able to help me. It kept me going and allowed me to continue to serve on camera with the PCC Production Team.

I never shared with anyone the fact that I felt physically miserable. Another one of Louie's messages, "Don't give the Enemy a seat at your table" spoke to me loud and clear. That's exactly what I was doing. I was letting him sit with me and feed me fear by the spoonful. I was in fear of being in debt forever, not being able to work production because NBA TV might not select me, and most importantly, I was in fear of failing as a husband and a father. None of this was good, and my effort to try to hide these things was not beneficial either. Jaci knew I wasn't feeling well but had no concept of the internal bed of nails I was experiencing. Why did I still struggle with control? I controlled my secret fears by keeping them hidden.

Even with my phone's screen saver set as "Don't give the Enemy a seat at your table" and serving almost every Sunday at Passion, I still struggled internally. I became a great actor at Passion, not letting anyone know that I was in such pain while filling up with anger and discontent. I started to look for, found, and pointed out every weakness in Jaci. Pornography in secret became even more of an escape. I knew I needed more than ever to be rescued again by God, but how? I had no right to ask for more. I was a fraud.

What I didn't realize at the time was this secret poison was slowly killing me, killing my relationships with Jaci and the kids, and killing my relationship with God. Let me be totally honest and transparent here: As you and I both know, God had already done so much for me, and what was I doing with it? Talk about a stubborn, hardheaded meathead. I was drowning in the Enemy's lies and darkness. I felt I absolutely had no business asking any of my teammates for help. Or asking God, for that matter. I was drowning alone in the darkness while everyone at Passion seemed to be celebrating victories.

When Christmas finally arrived, I looked forward to some good family time that might spark something in me to overcome what I was feeling. That morning as Jaci was busy in the kitchen making a good, old fashioned southern breakfast, I jumped into the shower and almost immediately felt intense chest pressure and discomfort. Since I had no numbness or jaw pain, I chose to just brush it off, get dressed, and take my meds. I decided a walk might help whatever this thing was, so I grabbed the dogs and headed out the door. I quickly realized the walk wasn't going to help, so I came back home right away. I sat on the front porch and enjoyed the sun, hoping for some relief. After 30 minutes, there were no signs of improvement.

I went inside to tell Jaci that she should probably call and cancel our Christmas plans with my mom and brother. I was in too much "back pain" to do anything. She gave me a look that questioned if I was being serious but got on the phone regardless. For some reason, this was the most honest I could get with her. I laid down on the bed and took some giant swigs of antacid to see if I could get some relief, but of course there was no relief to be had.

Jaci came and found me to see what was going on. She knew I wouldn't cancel Christmas unless I was seriously hurting. She asked me if we needed to go to the ER, followed with a little sales pitch about us being so close to the out-of-pocket maximum for the year that it wouldn't cost us much this week, but after the end of the year all that would change. That was all I needed to hear.

On the way to the hospital, I finally confessed it wasn't my back, rather it was chest pressure that just wouldn't go away. She scolded me for hiding that info for so long and got us to the ER fast, not as fast as I would have, but we didn't get a flat tire, so we were both glad about that.

Jaci dropped me off at the ER door with instructions to tell them I was having chest pain while she went to park the car. I walked in and told the receptionist exactly what I was supposed to say while including a compliment about her Christmas sweater. She thanked me and had me sign, print, and date the consent form while a nurse started getting my vitals. My blood pressure was seriously high, so I was immediately ushered to a room full of nurses and doctors all wearing their finest Christmas apparel. Within seconds, I was wearing an open hospital gown with IVs going in seemingly every vein. They started me on oxygen, Morphine for the pain, Nitroglycerin to open my blood vessels, and Heparin to prevent blood clots. As they handed me baby aspirin to chew to stop the formation of clots that could block blood flow to the heart, Jaci walked into this scene. She started answering all their questions, including correcting my valuation of my pain level. Jaci changed my valuation of seven to nine or ten, accurately adding the extra points I subtracted to look tough. By this point I could barely talk. I wasn't sure what was going on with me.

Over the next several hours, nausea and pain hit me so hard that every minute felt like an hour. I laid there just praying and repeating to myself that even if I wasn't okay, Jesus was.

I'm not okay... but Jesus is. I'm not okay... but Jesus is. I'm not okay...

A wave of grief hit me as I recognized that I had done this to myself. Following my first stent in 2012 to open my "widow-maker" artery, I had not suffered any lasting pain, pressure, or discomfort, so my serious lifestyle changes had not stuck. My diet had way too many Snickers bars in it, among many other things that were not good for me. On top of my bad eating habits, I hadn't been dealing with my stress appropriately. I tried my best to trust God with a new job, but my efforts to get us out of debt caused me to be a real grinch. I created a lot of tension by imposing a strict budget for Christmas presents. This wasn't good for me or my marriage.

I was admitted into the hospital on the cardiac care floor. When my kids came to see me, I didn't even try to put on a show for them by pretending I wasn't doing so badly. I was doing that badly, and I had no acting abilities left to speak of. Rachel asked to see my chart and the EKG results. She was enrolled in an anesthesiologist assistant master's program at the time. As a student, she had learned so much that she could ask intelligent questions and translate the doctor's thought processes. This did my (proverbial) heart well to see her so confident about all this intricate medical stuff. It seemed I was experiencing foreshadowing of her well into her career, bringing light into the darkness and helping soothe fear for patients who were facing the unknowns of surgery. DJ took it upon himself to fan me to keep me cooler. I felt like it was a thousand degrees in the room, and him wafting cool air on me gave me a load of relief. Having my two kids helping me, made a huge difference in my outlook.

My pain increased by the moment, as I grew more miserable, scared, and exhausted. Jaci stayed with me every painful second of this hospital adventure, and I was so thankful for her. My wife knew me so well that I didn't even have to say a word to her; she just knew what I was thinking and feeling. That, combined with her being one of the world's greatest pharmacists, helped me know I was in good hands. As my advocate, she analyzed every medication they put me on.

As the day turned ever so slowly into night, my condition worsened to more critical and life threatening. Jaci sat at my bedside and asked me if we could pray together. I whispered to her, "You should pray for both of us, please. I don't want to talk." Jaci asked God to give me peace and comfort while blessing the medical team with answers and solutions. She closed by asking for healing and strength. I thought that was all the right stuff to pray for, so I squeezed her hand to communicate a hearty thank you.

Throughout the night, the Cardiac team saw my troponin level go from 0.5 to 5.0, up to 13, and then all the way up to 57 (normal level range is 0.0 to 0.04). That qualifies as a major heart event, so I was moved to the Cardio ICU.

In the CICU, they could give a higher dose of medication to make sure I'd be ready for a heart catheterization as soon as possible, which happened at about 6:45 a.m. when a team of husky male medical staff came into the room to take me down to the heart cath lab. To be fair, I am not a skinny guy by anyone's standards, but did they need to send in the New York Giants offensive line to move me?

On the way to the lab, one of the linebackers looked down at me and said, "You must be someone very special. The head of Cardiology is coming in on his day off just to do your heart cath because the lab is completely booked today. That's great news for you, brother. He's so skilled he can open blockages in the lab that most other doctors would have to do through open heart surgery."

I couldn't keep my mouth shut over this revelation. "I am very blessed to be a son of God."

Every single member of the offensive line affirmed my statement. "Amen, brother."

When I woke up after the two-and-a-half-hour procedure, the surgeon told me that he found the original stent still in place and wide open. That was not the only good news. I was 100 percent blocked in two arteries and 75 percent in another. I had suffered two major heart attacks and survived. He had to insert three different stents to save my heart and my life. I was their "Christmas Miracle." The surgeon added that my heart had sustained significant damage, but he was hopeful I would soon feel a lot better and with prayers, possibly make a good recovery.

When I got back to my CICU room, I seemed to be experiencing the same, even worse symptoms than I was before my procedure. The chest pressure and nausea were still bad. I couldn't figure out why things weren't better. I told Jaci and my nurse as soon as they walked into the room. They assured me that I just needed to rest and that my body and heart would "reset." The floor doctor reminded us that troponin levels act like a bell curve; they have to go up before they can come down. Jaci gave me the extra reassurance that Rachel had been with the surgeon and was able to tell exactly what blood vessels were blocked and what he had done to save my life. It did make me feel better that everyone I trusted saw things the same way.

As the hours slowly passed by, seeming more like days, my chest pain and nausea were making me not only miserable, but also anxious. I was a giant mess. I thought maybe I was just "that guy" who couldn't be fixed so easily. Maybe my surgeon would need to go back in and do open heart surgery. How many more times am I going to have to go through this kind of trauma?

STOP.

This does me no good—it allows the Enemy to sit at my table and eat my food and put his feet up. It doesn't reflect an understanding that even when I'm not okay, Jesus is. By now I knew the only thing I could control was my thinking. I needed to lean on Him and try to find joy in this pain. Like Psalm 30:11 where God can turn my wailing into dancing and joy. The only problem was that I was scared.

Jaci is God's gift to me, and as I mentioned earlier, the world's greatest pharmacist. She was able to come up with a Hail Mary combination of three different drugs on my chart that just might give me some relief if they could all hit at the same time.

I sat in the chair as they administered the IV meds, what they called the "trifecta," and the next thing I remember was Jaci tapping me in the arm, telling me that I needed to move over to the bed since I had fallen asleep. That seemed highly unlikely to me, but I shuffled over to lay down while my nurse smiled big for the first time. I went right to sleep and woke up two and a half hours later feeling like a new, born-again man. No more pressure. No more pain. No more nausea. Unbelievable.

When I woke up, a nurse shift change had occurred. My new nurse, Taylor, was reading the report about all the insanity that had occurred that day. She looked at me with a big smile. "Are you TJ, the cameraman from Passion City Church? I think I remember you from when Pastor Brad (campus pastor) jumped up on your camera stand and talked about how faithfully you serve as one of the Door Holders." I was coherent enough to have an amazing conversation with her about serving at church and beyond. I couldn't believe that this is how this episode ends—feeling so close to death (yet again), and then getting an opportunity to have a spiritual conversation as soon as I turned the corner.

Of course, it would work out that way. It helped me realize that I can be okay ... because Jesus is okay. He is in control. Even if I had died that day in that hospital, I would have been okay.

I know that seems like a weird thing to say, and it is, really. But this current reality we are living in isn't as important as we think it is. If I had died, I *would have* been okay. More than okay, really. The reality of Heaven is so powerful and attractive. On Earth, moments like I had with Taylor, as we encouraged each other in being good servants, are the things that matter. That's the "Good Stuff." It's the relationships and the encouragement we give one another, and for me, the unconditional love of a woman that makes a difference.

There's a powerful part of Scripture that talks about this when it came to Jesus: In your relationships with one another, have the same mindset as Christ Jesus: Who, being in very nature God, did not consider equality with God something to be used to his own advantage; rather, he made himself nothing by taking the very nature of a servant, being made in human likeness. And being found in appearance as a man, he humbled himself by becoming obedient to death— even death on a cross! (Philippians 4:5-8)

Having the same mindset as Jesus seems rather impossible. I'm pretty convinced it is doable though, at least in part. You see, while Jesus was completely human, He was still completely God at the same time. It's a fancy theological concept called the hypostatic union. For some reason, even though He was equal with God the Father, He did not consider His equality as something to use for His benefit. It's quite remarkable, considering I personally carried a mindset of being equals, or more than equals, for as long as I can remember. That's what I was doing by taking control of everything—I viewed myself as more important than God. It's ridiculous when I state it out loud, but this is exactly what my viewpoint was. *If God cared or understood about me, He would get this right.* It always felt like I had to take over to make sure things went well.

Does this sound familiar? To be honest, I don't know anyone who hasn't struggled with viewing our *equality with God* (italics for sarcastic emphasis) as something to use to our advantage. It is, quite literally, the nature of the original sin. Adam and Eve thought equality with God was a good option for them. They liked the idea of having control.

Jesus made a different choice for Himself. He took on the very nature of a servant. As crazy as that sounds, if we read the Gospels with this viewpoint, we will struggle to see Jesus any other way. He came to serve us. The perfect Door Holder. Well, that is partly true. He came to serve His Father, who asked Him to serve us. What did that service look like? Well, obedience to death on a cross, on top of everything He did prior. It is quite remarkable how much He did during His three years of ministry, but then to give His life … for you and for me? It's absurd in all the very best ways.

If there is a single person who ever walked the face of the Earth who deserved to live with total control, it is Jesus. But He didn't. So, why should I? Why should I pursue equality over servanthood? The answer is, I shouldn't.

22

Deep Dive

But if we walk in the light, as he is in the light, we have fellowship with one another, and the blood of Jesus his Son cleanses us from all sin. (1 John 1:7, ESV)

BACK SAFE AND ALIVE IN our home, I knew for a fact I was not okay. I needed to make some major changes in my life, especially reducing stress and adjusting what I was eating and how much. Most importantly I needed to repair my relationship with God and my family.

As I sat resting on our front porch swing, reflecting on what I had just experienced, Rachel joined me with a hug and a kiss. She turned and looked me directly in my eyes.

"Daddy, it's time you stop living in hypocrisy and darkness. That stress is not meant for you to carry. Please be honest with yourself and us. Surrender everything to God."

Her words of truth cracked my heart wide open. My biggest stressor and heaviest burden had been not being true to myself and others, living in hypocrisy. Saying I was releasing control but still secretly holding onto it, sometimes in destructive ways.

In the weeks and months that followed, I took steps to get rid of items that took me away from spending time with God and my family. At the same time, I did a deep dive into my own darkness and addictions. I spent weeks talking openly with one of my accountability mentors about my control issues and my attraction to pornography. He helped me peel back the layers protecting my heart.

At one point he expressed how unworthy he felt to be my mentor and friend. He went on to tell me he had been raped several times by a family member when he was a little boy. In that moment, his revelation of childhood molestation unlocked the most traumatic childhood experience in my life. One I had compartmentalized and locked away. My friend's humble confession jolted my mind and unlocked a horrific, deeply buried memory that had caused me such shame as a boy.

A year or so before our National Championship Super Bowl, my neighbor started molesting me. As an 8-year-old boy, I thought our neighbor, a preacher's son, was a super cool teenager. I wanted to be just like him, to have his approval. So, his sudden interest in me, inviting me over to his house after school for snacks, made me feel accepted, even kind of cool like I thought he was. Over time, we started moving from his kitchen and living room to his bedroom to play music. Next thing I knew, our time together turned sexual. I was scared to death and confused. I couldn't tell anyone. Who would believe me over the preacher's son? Until that session with my accountability mentor, I had not shared this shameful secret with anyone, least of all my mother—who had actually saved me from this without realizing it. She had stepped in and unknowingly rescued me from my perpetrator by forcing me to come directly home from school for therapy. No more afternoon visits to the sexual abuse next door. As a little boy, I quickly buried those terrible memories so deeply that they remained hidden, even from myself, for decades. When my friend opened up in his own vulnerability to confess his childhood sexual abuse, my own shame was released.

My mentor and I discussed how, just like him, as a young boy I had lost all control, and how I had desperately wanted control back at any cost. The molestation, along with my dyslexia, became the foundation for my addiction to control everything and constantly seek approval from men. Unlocking the memory opened my eyes so I could deal with the deeper issue at its root.

What a blessing that years earlier, God had prompted my client and business mentor Cari to get me to attend the Choices seminar and then become a facilitator. One of the processes I led attendees through gave them back freedom and power after being a victim. When we repeatedly think about the pain of being a victim and what happened to us, we give the perpetrator the power to keep repeating the assault and to continue living in our heads rent free. In the process "Victim to Victor," we learned by first acknowledging what happened to us and then the pain of being a victim. Eventually we were able to move to forgiveness. And it is through the act of forgiveness that we regain control over the perpetrator and the freedom to yield that control to God to carry. Now as an adult, I have both the tools and loving support to deal with this newly unlocked revelation. It was time to gain freedom from another enemy that had taken control over me, even while I thought I'd had it under control.

When Dad passed away shortly after Jaci and I got married, I inherited his *Playboy* monthly subscription, much to Jaci's disappointment. After Rachel was born, I arrived home from work and Jaci was in the kitchen waiting for me with the new *Playboy*.

"Want to open your new *Playboy* for us to look at together?"

"Really? Sure," I said and proceeded to remove the outer wrapping. Jaci suggested I open it up to the centerfold layout, which I did. Then she said these words I will never forget, "Wow, she's beautiful. She's also someone's daughter just like yours." I closed the magazine and called *Playboy* to cancel my subscription. That was my own attempt at controlling my addiction. There were other ways to access porn, unfortunately, and I eventually found them.

Now, years later at age 60, pornography had long been a place where I went to escape stress and anxiety, to regain control. Porn was easy to access, and it fed my thirst for control. Ultimately, pornography damaged my own children as well as my marital relationship with Jaci.

I didn't know until recently how much damage my pornography habit had caused our beautiful daughter. She wrote me a letter that tore my heart out of my chest. Within the seven handwritten pages, she revealed her own personal struggles with anxiety brought on by my porn addiction. She went on to share how, as an eight-year-old little girl, she had sneaked into my basement office. Unbeknownst to me, she stood behind me and watched girl-on-girl porn on my computer screen over my shoulder. I had no idea she was there. *What? What kind of father does that to his own child?* The inappropriate images scarred Rachel's innocent, tender mind. She was the same age I was when my neighbor sexually molested me. In her letter, she acknowledged how much she has struggled with anxiety, especially during grad school, brought on by seeing the sickening porn as a child. Thankfully, Rachel, now 26 years old, took this anxiety seriously and after much prayer reached out to a Christian counselor for help. After several sessions, she discovered that most of her anxiety came from her being "imprinted" by the porn she had seen as a little girl. She wanted me to know how hard she has worked and prayed so that today she struggles less with anxiety. She also wanted me to know she had forgiven me. By acknowledging, forgiving, and then yielding to God the control that anxiety had over her, she moved from victim to victor.

I hit my knees, and with tears in my eyes, I begged God to forgive me for what I had done and help restore my relationships with my family. I desperately needed God's forgiveness and restoration. I had allowed the Enemy, pornography, and lust to come between me and Jaci and between me and my kids. Most importantly, my attraction to porn to feel in control had come between me and God. I wasn't fooling anyone, especially Jaci and the kids, who had continued to pray that God would heal me from my addictions to control and to pornography and bring me back to be the man God intended. It was now time for me to get real and do the same hard work to repair my relationships with Jaci, Rachel, and Daniel.

As I poured out my soul to God, I felt a giant weight being lifted off my heart. This feeling of freedom gave me the courage to sit down with Jaci and the kids and make a complete confession.

I started by saying how much I regretted allowing pornography to destroy our lives. I assured them I would be blocking every and any access to pornography on my phone and computer, which I did. Then, with brokenness and humility, I described how my friend had helped me go into the darkness of my past to unwrap my darkest secret, a place of shame that I had compartmentalized and locked away decades ago. I shared with my wife and my children how I had been molested as a young boy. This was in no way an excuse for what I had done, but it was a critical factor that added up to feeding my control issues that had caused so much damage. God touched each one of us as I confessed my sins to my wife and children and asked them for forgiveness. In that special time of openness, years of damage began to heal, and I too moved from victim to victor, yielding control to God.

With my renewed commitment, I decided to get re-baptized. Baptism is such a big deal in our faith lives. If I were to sum up the point of baptism, it would be to surrender ourselves to Christ, trusting that He has a plan for us in this lifetime and beyond. Another way to say it: We die to the concept of wielding control ourselves and choose to yield control to Christ.

While going through a Bible Study called Launch at Passion, several of us made the decision to recommit our lives to Jesus. Now as adults with a personal relationship with Him, we again accepted Him as our savior. Then each of us added our own personal lightbulb to the giant "Jesus is Life" wall board in the oval. A few weeks later, as a group, we got baptized on the same Sunday. Many of us, including me, were baptized as a child, yet collectively, we felt like that wasn't reflective of us yielding control to Jesus. As children, we didn't get any say on the matter. But now we had free will and a choice: Are we going to wield or yield?

When we wield something, we hold it and use it like a weapon. That bank robber was wielding a gun up against my head, and he did so to demonstrate his power over me. It worked in the short run, but he got caught eventually and was put in jail. So, there is a good argument against the wielding of something—it often catches up with us. We weren't meant to wield things. We have certainly learned to as a society, but it hasn't benefited us.

The most common weapon we have wielded is that of control. I have no doubt struggled with this, and I honestly believed I had good reason to. The odds were stacked against me when it came to living a successful life. My dyslexia and ADHD were not understood in the school system at the time. It was easier to write me off with the label of "broken" than it was to attempt to help me. Being molested as a child by a preacher's son set me up with all kinds of confusion and hurt. As a boy and a young man, if I didn't grab hold of control, waving it around like a mad man, what chance would I have? Of course, now I can see clearly that I would have been in better hands if I had yielded control to God earlier.

As I reflect on all this stuff in my story, I realize something very important about my efforts to wield control. The reason I worked so hard and franticly in so many ways was because I just wanted to be good. I wanted other people to know that I was good. If I could just be good enough, I would make it. So many things in my life made me feel bad. Dyslexia was at the top of the list. I didn't want to be bad—I wanted to be good. Actually, I wanted to be great. This is where my concept of God collides with my humanity. For the longest time, I thought Jesus came to make bad people good. That was the narrative I had always been told, so it was what I believed. The truth is slightly different.

God, being rich in mercy, because of the great love with which He loved us, even when we were dead in our trespasses, made us alive together with Christ—by grace you have been saved—and raised us up with Him and seated us with Him in the heavenly places in Christ Jesus, so that in the coming ages He might show the immeasurable riches of His grace in kindness toward us in Christ Jesus. (Ephesians 2:4-7, ESV)

Jesus did not come to make bad people good. He came to make dead people alive.

When baptism Sunday arrived, I gathered with my buddies to publicly declare our surrender to God. As each of us came up out of the water, we celebrated and cheered on one another. It was like winning the National Championship Super Bowl, except hundreds of times better! I think about that experience often, especially when I am tempted to wield control again. It is easy to do, often without much thought at all. But it is not better. Frankly, wielding control has always caused me to be bitter, not better.

As part of my post-baptism commitment, I must work to worry less and have more faith. I realize I need to spend more time in His Word and with my fellow production teammates. I am working to create better habits each day by opening my Bible or listening to messages and podcasts online. My heart is refreshed every time I get the opportunity to share my journey with others. I repeat the truth to myself daily: I have been forgiven and restored by God. I am a product of grace.

Rachel's letter sits on my desk as a constant reminder of forgiveness and restoration.

23

Choose to Yield

"For I know the plans I have for you," declares the Lord, "plans for welfare and not for evil, to give you a future and a hope." (Jeremiah 29:11, ESV)

TAKE IT FROM A CONTROL freak: It is not worth it to hang on to control. It gets us nowhere except in trouble of our own making.

To be clear, I am not saying to lie down on the ground and do absolutely nothing. What I am saying is that we can, and should, take time to figure out what it would look like to trust that Jesus is in control. I grew up hearing the old saying, "God gave you a rowboat and oars, now you need to paddle like hell to shore." I always wanted to be that guy, using what God gave me to go where I wanted to go. What I have learned over the years from doing just that, is a little different. God gave me a rowboat and oars, and now I need to have the faith that God's current will take me where He wants me to go. Another mic drop to yield control. He consistently provides answers and pathways, especially when we seek it. I can tell you with certainty that my business would have been way more successful had I learned how to yield control of it and trust the One who can control things.

I know this sounds like taking your hands off the steering wheel while you are speeding down the highway in hopes that "Jesus takes the wheel." That's not exactly what I am talking about. Besides, that bridge embankment is a sturdy object to hit head on. Yielding control in this analogy looks like asking Christ to navigate our turns. Should I go left, right, straight, or turn around? He will take control and guide us.

I have begun to experience this in real ways. For example, He "GPSed" me to these new friends at Passion City, and my life is immeasurably better because of them. And not only my life, but my family's lives as well.

Rachel shared with me not long ago, "Dad, the single most impactful thing you ever did for our family was to start attending Passion City Church." She proclaimed how Passion, namely Louie Giglio and Ben Stuart, had challenged her spiritually and gotten her to really dive into God's word. At Passion she also met Jay and Katherine Wolf and has read all their books. She went on to share how much she loves the Passion Band and hearing David Crowder for the first time. On a more personal note, she discovered she was not alone with her anxiety, as Louie also struggles with the same and has written several books about his struggles. Her favorites are *Putting an X Through Anxiety* and *Don't Give the Enemy a Seat at Your Table.*

Today, both of our kids are out on their own, working at jobs they love, and getting to bless others daily. The best part for me, they live close by and with their adult "free will," still choose to stop by weekly. I've gotten to know both our kids as adults, and they in turn have gotten to know Dad 2.0 who has a new lease on life and is a true product of grace. Daniel and I have gotten to spend a lot of time together working on several yard projects and just having fun at our neighborhood pool. Rachel stops by several times a week to walk with friends and attend Bible study. Jaci and I continue to work on our marriage and repair the damage porn caused. We have attended several marriage retreats at Chick-fil-A's WinShape Retreats at Berry College in Rome, Georgia, and even became a Host Couple to keep us dialed in to God's calling for us.

I used to think that God keeps a ledger book about us. That every time you do something, He sits there watching intently, waiting to make His judgment: Was that action going to get marked down in the left column as something bad, or would He make a mark on the good, right side because we did what Jesus would have done? Then after we had lived long enough, He would take us up and give a report on our record, and if we had enough marks on the right side, He would tell us, "Well done, good and faithful servant," and the pearly gates would open as a choir of angels began to float around in perfect harmonious surround-sound as we proudly strutted into Heaven.

I think we all desperately want this narrative to be true, but at the same time we want the threshold to be 51 percent on the good side, nothing more. I honestly believed the reason God hadn't "taken me home" during one of the multiple times that it seemed like I was a goner was because I hadn't quite gotten to the 51 percent mark. This is what grace felt like—Him giving me more time to improve the scoreboard. The problem is that the Old Testament succinctly tells us that the threshold is 100 percent if that's the game we are playing.

I know I haven't been successful when I've tried to be perfect. My efforts always had me wielding control like a weapon and was never, ever going to earn me the right to hear "Thorold Joseph, well done, good and faithful servant."

Thankfully, this isn't the way things work. Jesus came to make dead people, like me, alive. Not just humanly alive, although I would be foolish to think He wasn't a part of that in my story. He also came to make me spiritually alive.

I'll say it again: Jesus came and made me alive!

If that is true for me, it can be true for you. It simply takes yielding control. I know how easy it is to say that, and how hard it is to do. But it is better to surrender to Jesus, so much better. This is why I wanted, needed, to share my story. I needed to share it while I still had a chance. Who knows how the next medical emergency is going to end. I don't know how today is going to end, and that is okay because Jesus is okay (way more than okay, really). I can trust Him and yield total control to Him. I hope you choose to do the same as well, no matter what circumstances you are facing.

As I've said before, I realize that most of my life I acted like Peter from the Bible. Like Peter, I was a believer at heart, but one who questioned, doubted, and even complained a lot. When opportunities came up for me to affirm Jesus, I denied, refused, or stayed quiet much of the time. At times, I saw life as a glass half empty. I felt persecuted, forced to deal with one unfair struggle after another.

Now that I have journeyed a little farther through life, I've slowly changed my lens to see more like Paul. I recognize that God is into everything. I'm not as focused on negative situations, pain, or separation. I can see the value and good in situations where I could never see it before. Jesus loves me; I am alive because of Him. Despite my challenges with dyslexia, sexual child abuse, pornography, and control, I am a beautiful, wonderful child of God. And so are you.

These days I can write with a spirit of gratitude, having learned to finally, at last, truly, *so help me, God* ... let go and let God be in control.

Anthems *(Recommended Resources)*

THESE BOOKS AND FOUR FAVORITE songs—my "Anthems"—help me focus more on God and less on me. They trace my journey of discovering that *God is in total control.* It does not matter what others say; God knows the real me and loves me. God is into everything, every heartbeat of my heart, every detail.

1. *The 4:8 Principal,* by Tommy Newberry (Tyndale House Publishers, 2007)
2. *Winning the War on Worry*, by Louie Giglio (Thomas Nelson, 2022)
3. *The Suffering Guy*, by Jim Barnard (Independently published, 2021)

- *The Purpose Driven Life,* by Rick Warren (Zondervan, 2002)
- *Don't Give the Enemy a Seat at Your Table,* by Louie Giglio (Thomas Nelson, 2021)
- *Goliath Must Fall,* by Louie Giglio (Thomas Nelson, 2017)
- *Putting an X Through Anxiety,* by Louie Giglio (Passion Publishing 2023)
- *The Comeback,* by Louie Giglio (W Publishing, 2017)
- *Suffer Strong,* by Katherine and Jay Wolf (Zondervan, 2020)
- *Launching a Leadership Revolution,* by Chris Brady & Orrin Woodward (Business Plus, 2007)
- "More Like Jesus" – Passion
- "God Only Knows" – For King & Country
- "Everything" – TobyMac
- "Do It Again" – Elevation Worship

Acknowledgments

THE MESSAGE OF THIS BOOK has been marinating deep inside me for years, and it took acts of God and an entire village of some awesome people to help make it come alive.

To my wife, Jaci, thank you for being the love of my life, my best friend and constant encourager, especially in my darkest moments. Most of all thank you for your faith and helping me say what I mean.

To our kids, Rachel and Daniel, thank you for being the wonderful gifts you each are, sharing my journey and being bright lights for me. I'm blessed to be your dad.

To Kathryn and Lee Cushman, your long-time friendship has meant the world to Jaci and me. Katie, your willingness to give my very rough manuscript a read opened an amazing new world for me. Your belief in my words gave me the strength to continue and not give up on myself.

To Jay and Katherine Wolf, thank you both for your mentoring and encouragement to me on this journey and introducing me to Jim Barnard. Your openness and honesty in sharing your own struggles and darkness have been a constant light for me and my entire family. Thank you both for sharing your story of Hope. I've discovered that this world "does work for me" when I let go of control and trust God.

Also, a big thank you for my newest best friend, Jim "The Suffering Guy" Barnard, who took on my writing like a tiger hungry for raw truth [meat?]. Jim, Alisha, and Anderson, thank you for coming along on this most amazing journey with me. Alisha, your grace, willingness to share Jim, and strength through the toughest of times have blessed me and my family far more than you will ever know. Anderson, thank you for sharing your dad with me. Jim, your awesome smile, quick wit, and empowering words are the fuel that burns within my heart to share Jesus's stories. Not to mention your heavenly gift of untangling my words and reeling in my off-tangent rants. You are my brother forever.

To my Passion City Church and Production Team, thank you for always lifting me up and praying for my journey. Your hearts and friendships are such a blessing and bright light for me. I will continue to be honest and transparent with you.

To my mom and dad, thank you for being with me throughout my entire life and being wonderful examples of unconditional love. You are each a blessing and reminder of where I come from.

To my brothers, Jack and Bobby, thanks for making the journey so full of fun and excitement. I'm the man I am thanks to our relationships and childhood. I love you, Bros. To Janet, thank you for being my amazing big sis; thanks for your patience, grace, and for loving me anyway. You are always there for us.

And finally, to our dear friend, editor, and collaborator, Kathy Groom, thank you for helping me to dig even deeper and for guiding me along the right track as my book came to life. You are family, and you have blessed my entire family.

Food for Thought

National Champion Super Bowl

- Have you ever asked God, "If you love me, how could you let this happen to me?" or "Why would you make junk like me?" or "Why am I broken?"
- Have you ever felt you no longer belonged here or that the world wasn't going to work for you?
- Did you face trauma in your childhood home that was beyond your control? How did you cope with it?
- What was it like to repeat a grade or move to a new school?

> *Count it all joy, my brothers, when you meet trials of various kinds, for you know that the testing of your faith produces steadfastness. And let steadfastness have its full effect, that you may be perfect and complete, lacking in nothing.* (James 1:2-4, ESV)

Not so Good Things

- What sort of student were you? Was school carefree and fun or scary and at times overwhelming?
- What was it like for you, or someone you know, to have learning issues or speaking struggles speaking in front of others? How did you react?

- Were you or someone you love ever labeled as retarded, learning challenged, or other negative labels? How did that make you feel then? How about now?

> *You made me; you created me. Now give me the sense to follow your commands.* (Psalm 119:73, NLT)

All About Me

- Did your family attend church regularly? How did this affect your spiritual development?
- Growing up, how did it feel to have or not have your parents attend activities?
- Was there an adult who took time to build good character into you? Who?
- Did you ever build things or spend special times with a parent growing up? How did this, or the lack of this, impact you?

> *"Ah, stubborn children," declares the Lord, "who carry out a plan, but not mine."* (Isaiah 30:1a, ESV)

Real Deal

- Have you ever felt trapped, spiraling out of control? Did you turn to God and trust His plan for your life, or double down to take control?
- Have struggles drawn you closer or pushed you away from God?
- Has there been a time God showed you He was orchestrating your life, surprising you with circumstances that you did not earn or deserve?

- What is your relationship with Jesus like now?

> *The heart of man plans his way, but the Lord establishes his steps.* (Proverbs 16:9, ESV)

Change of Plans

- Did your lifelong dreams and plans ever fall apart?
- Did you blame God?
- Did you pray about the situation? What did you pray? How did things work out?
- Share an experience when someone seemed to limit what you could do. How did you respond? What happened? Do you still have scars or pain from that?

> *A man's steps are from the LORD; how then can man understand his way?* (Proverbs 20:24, ESV)

Mic Drop

- Have you ever experienced a time when you saw no way, no hope, and no answers, and then everything fell into place? Did you thank God or chalk it up to hard work and perseverance?
- Can you identify people God has put in your life for a specific purpose? Have you thanked them? Have you thanked God?
- Do others' negative comments or posts about you fire you up, making you stronger and more determined to prove them wrong? Or do they crush you?

> *O my God, in you I trust; let me not be put to shame; let not my enemies exult over me.* (Psalm 25:2, ESV)

Bold Enough

- Were you ever surprised by a promotion or a time someone recognized you in front of others? How did you feel?
- Was this your plan working or God's plan?
- What is a strong suit in your life, something you do well? When did you discover this talent? How did you develop it or who helped you develop it? How has it affected your growth and your life choices? Has it helped compensate for areas where you seem to lack ability?
- Do you see this ability as a gift from God? Have you seen Him use it for His purposes?

> *Hope deferred makes the heart sick, but a longing fulfilled is a tree of life.* (Proverbs 13:12, NIV)

Determined Pursuit

- Did you ever ask for permission to marry someone or ask for a big promotion?
- Did you ever meet the "right" girl or guy at the "wrong" time? What happened?
- Did you ever hear a small voice say, "they're the one?" What was that like? How did it turn out? Or is this an area of longing?
- Share a moment when you knew God was working for you, for your best interest.

> *You have captivated my… heart with one glance of your eyes ….* (Song of Solomon 4:9, ESV)

Beginnings and Endings

- Do you regularly sit down as a family to eat, talk, and pray?
- Have you experienced the loss of a baby or child or someone very dear to you?
- How did this impact your life? Did you blame God or someone else?

> *"I am the Alpha and the Omega, the First and the Last, the Beginning and the End."* (Revelation 22:13, NIV)

Out of Control

- Have you ever been in a life-threatening situation or lost all control? Did you freak out, pray, or what?
- Have you struggled with infertility? How did it impact your marriage and intimacy?
- Do you trust God for His plan for your life? Do your choices reflect that trust?

> *Unless the LORD builds a house, its builders labor in vain. Unless the LORD watches over the city, the watchmen stand guard in vain.* (Psalm 127:1, NIV)

Nothing if Not Persistent

- Have you experienced or been blessed by a miracle? What was it like to share it with others?
- TJ strove to meet up to his dad's success. Is there a person or model you strive to meet up to?
- When did you first accept that God is in control? Or have you

not accepted this yet?

> *See, I am doing a new thing! Now it springs up; do you not perceive it? I am making a way in the wilderness and streams in the wasteland.* (Isaiah 43:19, NIV)

More than I Knew

- Have you ever attended a service or a conference that gave you a whole new perspective? Were you reluctant to go? What or who persuaded you?
- Have you/do you have a mentor in your life who spoke the truth about you that you needed to hear?
- Do you have a fear of failure? What is it you most fear? What is the worst that could happen to you?

> *And what do you benefit if you gain the whole world but lose your own soul? Is anything worth more than your soul?* (Matthew 16:26, NLT)

Disappointed and Doubtful

- Create your own Gripe List and Gratitude List. What did you learn from your lists?
- Are you more inclined to share the gripes or the gratefuls?
- Do you live with a controller? How do you react?

> *Therefore, if anyone is in Christ, he is a new creation; the old has gone; the new has come!* (2 Corinthians 5:17, NIV)

It's About Time

- Have you ever been completely dependent upon others to survive?
- Have you ever struggled with anxiety or fear or had suicidal thoughts?
- How are you with asking for help?
- Have you surrendered an unhealthy situation to God? What was the outcome?

> *Humble yourselves, therefore, under God's mighty hand, that He may lift you up in due time.* (1 Peter 5:6, NIV)

Big Deal or Not

- Did you experience moments you knew only God could have made this happen?
- Have you ever asked God for something, and He granted it? Or didn't grant it? What was the outcome?
- Have you ever denied God's work? How do you feel about that?

> *I shall not die, but I shall live, and recount the deeds of the Lord.* (Psalm 118:17, ESV)

The Whole Time

- When did you expect a "toy" to make you happy and confident? Did it?
- Have you ever lost everything and had to start over? What was the result?
- Have you ever bargained with God? What happened?

> *Jesus said to him, "Get up, take up your bed and walk."* (John 5:8, ESV)

Stubborn Man's Attention

- How would your spouse say you are doing as a parent?
- Have you experienced starting to go to church or resuming going after a time away? How did you go about searching for a church? What drew you to where you are?
- How do you approach your work and your co-workers? To what degree are you driven to control?
- Did God ever have you do something you normally wouldn't do, only to blow your mind later with His plan?

> *In the same way, let your light shine before others, so that they may see your good works and give glory to your Father who is in heaven.* (Matthew 5:16, ESV)

Dyslexia is Not a Curse

- Have any of your own personal fears or traumas rubbed off on your spouse or children?
- How do you help your children deal with their fears or failures?

- Have you ever had to make a sizeable investment in your or your children's education, or make a big change without the resources immediately in hand? What happened?

> *And we know that God causes everything to work together for the good of those who love God and are called according to his purpose for them.* (Romans 8:28, NLT)

Swag, Not Swagger

- Have your children ever spoken truth into your heart?
- Have you ever been surprised by how your child reacted to a negative situation or a struggle that you as a child had trouble with and handled poorly?
- Are you working on becoming a servant leader for your family? How?
- What's a book you've read lately that improved your life?

> *Have I not commanded you? Be strong and courageous. Do not be terrified; do not be discouraged, for the Lord your God will be with you wherever you go.* (Joshua 1:9, NIV)

Door Holder

- Have you shared a talent that you consider to be small, but God used in a bigger way?
- What is your current church involvement?
- What is a simple way you could be a Door Holder?

> *Having gifts that differ according to the grace given to us, let us use them.* (Romans 12:6, ESV)

I'm Not Okay, but Jesus Is

- Have you or a loved one suffered a medical event like a heart attack from which you or they were not expected to recover?
- Has God ever spoken to you? What was that like?
- Have you been ashamed of who you are, afraid that people won't love the real you?
- What do you struggle with in the darkness?

> *Submit yourselves, then, to God. Resist the devil, and he will flee from you.* (James 4:7, NIV)

Deep Dive

- Can you remember a time God spoke to you through someone's story, unlocking a piece of your own story that you had locked away?
- Are there places where you need to step out of the darkness and into the light? Are there people you need to forgive? Or ask for forgiveness? Will you?
- Could you be someone's "I've also been in the darkness; you're not alone"?

> *But if we walk in the light, as he is in the light, we have fellowship with one another, and the blood of Jesus his Son cleanses us from all sin.* (1 John 1:7, ESV)

Choose to Yield

- Do you find it hard to ask for help? Why? Is there someone in your life or in your church who could help you?
- Have tragedies in your life ever ended up being blessings? Can you relate these experiences to yielding control?
- Has TJ's story helped you identify and yield in your own tendencies to be a control freak? Or helped you relate to a loved one who is?

> *"For I know the plans I have for you," declares the Lord, "plans for welfare and not for evil, to give you a future and a hope."* (Jeremiah 29:11, ESV)

About the Author

TJ Sharitz serves as a paraprofessional, mentoring and supporting high school students with dyslexia, social anxieties, and emotional and behavioral disorders. In addition, he works for various video broadcasting companies as a consultant, camera operator, and production specialist. TJ has over twenty years' experience as a successful business owner in the diverse franchise advertising/marketing and broadcast production fields. He holds a BA degree in Communications Studies from Virginia Polytechnic Institute and State University (VA Tech).

TJ's serves on the Passion City Church, Browns Bridge Church, and Decatur City Church Video Production Teams. He has also served as a church community group leader, Purpose Driven Life facilitator, and a servant leadership coach. He and his wife, Jaci, enjoy serving as a host couple at WinShape Marriage Retreats. TJ considers his life purpose to be Simply Empowering.

TJ and Jaci live north of Atlanta close to Lake Lanier with their two dogs, Dak, a Rottweiler, and a brindle boxer named Layla. They love having both of their grown kids living close by and hosting Sunday night family dinners.

For more resources visit ControlFreakLVP.com or TJSharitz.com.

Made in the USA
Columbia, SC
02 August 2024